C000081338

Raise a Standard
for the Nations

Go and Make Disciples

Book IV of the Barnabas Series
Cho Larson

WHP
Warner Howe Press

Albertville, AL

Published by Warner House Press of Albertville, Alabama USA

Copyright © 2024 Cho Larson
Cover Design and Illustration © 2024 Ian Loudon, OKAY Media
Interior Design © 2024 Warner House Press

All rights reserved. No part of this book may be used or reproduced in any manner whatsoever without written permission, except in the case of brief quotations in critical articles and reviews. For more information, contact

Warner House Press
1325 Lane Switch Road
Albertville, Alabama 35951
USA

Published 2024
Printed in the United States of America

Cover image used under license from Shutterstock.com.

Unless otherwise noted, all scripture quotations are taken from HOLY BIBLE, NEW INTERNATIONAL VERSION®. Copyright © 1973, 1978, 1984 by International Bible Society. Used by permission of Zondervan Publishing House.

Scripture quotations marked ESV are from The ESV® Bible (The Holy Bible, English Standard Version®), © 2001 by Crossway, a publishing ministry of Good News Publishers. Used by permission. All rights reserved.

Scripture quotations marked NLT are from the Holy Bible, New Living Translation, Copyright © 1996, 2004, 2007, 2013, 2015 by Tyndale House Foundation. Used by permission of Tyndale House Publishers Inc., Carol Stream, Illinois 60188. All rights reserved.

26 25 24 23 1 2 3 4 5

ISBN: 978-1-951890-55-1

Dedicated to
Andrew
"Nowhere to lay his head."

Contents

Your Bible Adventure Begins Here

Do church outreach programs leave you feeling defeated? You're encouraged to witness, invite your neighbors to church, and testify to coworkers, but the results are often discouraging. Because of disappointing results, churches often replace the work of the Great Commission with ministries that can show trackable and measurable results.

Isaiah's words, "He will raise a banner for the nations"[1] are inspirational, a great visual, and a good mission's motto, but what does this look like in practice? The task before us is monumental. The earth's population is over eight billion people, and there are 385,000 more babies born every day. Reaching all of them is an impossible task for one person or one local church. We face a greater challenge today because the light of Christ has been hidden from this generation. Gen X, Y, and Z have little or no knowledge of their Creator. The only forgiveness they've heard about is for student loans.

Where do we begin, and how is it possible to finish the mountain-sized task Jesus commanded us to accomplish? Church outreach budgets are underfunded. The church is understaffed. Volunteers are hard to come by. So, what are we to do? How can we be faithful in this work and be a banner raiser with the full measure of the blessings of Christ?

Never discount small beginnings. Take a little step and start training disciples. This is the job of everyone in the church. We're called to teach and prepare people to go to neighbors and nations to serve as ambassadors of Christ and the cross. We disciple those who gather as a church so they can confidently proclaim Jesus' life-giving death until He comes again.

Ambassadors need to have knowledge of this great salvation so they can proclaim Christ to their coworkers and the family next door. Messengers of the cross need to be equipped to defend their faith to the guys when they play basketball in the driveway. When we take visiting family out fishing for salmon, we need to know how to fish for lost souls. We must send witnesses of this great salvation with a zeal that comes from the knowledge of Christ's forgiveness and saving grace. The following chapters are a fishing guide presented verse by verse to strengthen and inspire Christians to accomplish the task of proclaiming Christ's saving graces. This good work is only possible in the power of the Spirit of Christ and the authority of Jesus' holy name.

---

1 Isaiah 11:12.

Raise a Banner for the Nations is the fourth book of the Barnabas series. The lesson plans build on the tenants of the preceding Bible study guides, *The Mystery of Christ in You* (book one), *Build a House for My Name* (book two), and *Ascend to Mount Zion* (book three).

> "Not by might nor by power, but by my Spirit," says the Lord Almighty. "What are you, mighty mountain? Before Zerubbabel you will become level ground. Then he will bring out the capstone to shouts of 'God bless it! God bless it!'" (Zechariah 4:6–7)

Part I

Fields Ready for Harvest

"I tell you, open your eyes and look at the fields! They are ripe for harvest." (John 4:35)

The work of the gospel is to bring lost souls into the saving grace and comfort of God's eternal promises. The time is short, and we must be alert and apply ourselves to the call of Jesus' Great Commission.

Chapter 1: Pray for the Harvest

Key Scriptures:

- "He told them, 'The harvest is plentiful, but the workers are few. Ask the Lord of the harvest, therefore, to send out workers into his harvest field'" (Luke 10:2).

- "As for other matters, brothers and sisters, pray for us that the message of the Lord may spread rapidly and be honored, just as it was with you. And pray that we may be delivered from wicked and evil people, for not everyone has faith" (2 Thessalonians 3:1–2).

A successful harvest requires everyone to pitch in and help. Crews show up just before sunrise to toil in the fields, while others work to keep the machinery running, and still others serve by feeding the workers good, healthy food. Even Grandpa gets in the act, telling them how they harvested in the good old days. When the Lord of the harvest summons us to this good work, He calls every Christian to do their part. One of the most essential jobs is that of a prayer warrior.

Every good work we begin in God's kingdom must begin the same way that Paul and Barnabas established the churches in Lystra, Iconium, and Antioch. They began with prayer, fasting, committing themselves to the Lord, and trusting Him for all they needed to accomplish the work He commanded them to do.

A prayer according to Galatians 6:9:

Heavenly Father, strengthen us by your Spirit and Word so that we will not become weary in well doing as we prepare for the day when we will reap a bountiful harvest.

Prayer is an excellent way to start our day. A prayer of faith while waiting on the Lord is a great way to begin every good work. We can't go forward and reach our goal without devoted prayer warriors to back us up. We must look up to the Throne of Grace and call out with fervent and effective petitions, because our help comes from the Lord.[1]

When we seek for and wait upon our heavenly Father with fasting and prayer, He opens the way to effective ministry and service. The anointing, gifting, and empowering work of the Holy Spirit that is necessary for the work of the harvest is poured out upon those who ask. Doors of ministry opportunity are

---

1 Psalm 121:2.

thrown open to those who first gather to pray in agreement with each other and in accord with God's Word.

> *Hear my cry for help, my King and my God, for to you I pray. In the morning, Lord, you hear my voice; in the morning I lay my requests before you and wait expectantly.* (Psalm 5:2–3)

A season of repentant prayer and fasting changes hearts and minds and fills God's people with a Christ-like attitude. Do you want the desire of God's heart to be the desire of your heart? Confess the wrong desires you have held onto and turn to the Lord with a contrite heart. God is faithful, just, forgiving, and overflows with mercy. He abounds with love to all who call upon Him.[2]

Through repentance and rest, your heavenly Father rescues you when your feet slip from His narrow pathway.[3] In quietness and trust there is strength to take up your cross and lift high Christ's banner of love for all nations. First, confess your wrongs and then confess the sins of the church as you prepare for the work of the harvest. Turn from your sins and then the heavens, once like iron, open to your heart's cry.[4]

> *So I turned to the Lord God and pleaded with him in prayer and petition, in fasting, and in sackcloth and ashes. I prayed to the Lord my God and confessed: "Lord, the great and awesome God, who keeps his covenant of love with those who love him and keep his commandments, we have sinned and done wrong. We have been wicked and have rebelled; we have turned away from your commands and laws. We have not listened to your servants the prophets, who spoke in your name to our kings, our princes and our ancestors, and to all the people of the land.* ((Daniel 9:3–6)

There's more to repentant prayers than simply saying, "Oh, sorry, Lord." That may be a good beginning, but true repentance comes from a broken and contrite heart. When sin becomes systemic, church leaders ought to call for a sacred assembly to lead the people in repentance. Remember that we are rarely alone in our sin. Sin is contagious. It affects everyone around us. Widespread dishonor of God's holy name calls for the redeemed to stop what they're doing and repent from their hearts. This is more than a "repeat after me" kind of prayer. This is the Spirit of Christ flooding God's sons and daughters who come together so our hearts may be pierced with grief.

> *Blow the trumpet in Zion, declare a holy fast, call a sacred assembly. Gather the people, consecrate the assembly.* (Joel 2:15–16)

---

2 Psalm 86:5.
3 Isaiah 30:15.
4 Leviticus 26:19, Deuteronomy 28:23, 1 Peter 3:7.

When the church sends workers out into the harvest field, we must not send them in their own strength, because the job before them is impossible on their own. If they go out to speak their own words and attempt to do the job with common, God-given talents and abilities, they'll fail miserably.

Every worker in the church who contributes to the work of the harvest needs to be set apart with prayer and fasting for the work they are called to accomplish. The janitor, Sunday school teacher, greeters, parking lot attendants, as well as pastors and missionaries need to be set apart for their job by a fasting, prayerful, and worshipping church. We are called to fast, pray, and seek the Lord and then lay hands on them to impart the gifting and empowering Holy Spirit upon them before we appoint them to a task in God's kingdom.

While they were worshiping the Lord and fasting, the Holy Spirit said, "Set apart for me Barnabas and Saul for the work to which I have called them."
(Acts 13:2)

Paul and Barnabas gave us a pattern for establishing a new church with strong spiritual leaders. They tested men to be sure their trust in the Lord was solid. They checked their spiritual strength by asking them to first serve in lesser capacities. They tested potential church leaders to be sure they were maturing in the faith.[5] The apostles observed workers to be sure they were temperate, gentle, and good financial stewards.[6] If they had servant-like attitudes, Paul and Barnabas fasted and prayed to seek the Lord before appointing them to serve as deacons and elders in the church. They laid hands on the leaders to anoint them by the Holy Spirit for the spiritual gifts necessary to accomplish their noble tasks.

Paul and Barnabas appointed elders for them in each church and, with prayer and fasting, committed them to the Lord, in whom they had put their trust.
(Acts 14:23)

When we proclaim the true gospel and lift up Jesus Christ, we raise a banner to gather all who will come. They'll come en masse to receive sweet words of saving grace they've never heard before. They press in because they're burdened and without hope, wanderers without light to guide them.

Wherever the true gospel is proclaimed, look up and you will see a plentiful harvest of lost souls in need of Christ. If the church is unwilling to fast and pray for workers in the harvest, there will be too few. The church is called to prepare people to serve in the harvest fields that loom before us like fields of golden grain.

First we strengthen the weak, sick, and wounded among us. Then we search for those who wandered away and bring back the strays.[7] With gentle loving care, we bring them back into the Good Shepherd's fold. Then, the church dis-

---

5 1 Timothy 3:6.
6 1 Timothy 3:3.
7 Ezekiel 34:4—6.

ciples them so they may go out as ambassadors to our neighbors, our hometown, and people in far-off lands.

> *When he saw the crowds, he had compassion on them, because they were harassed and helpless, like sheep without a shepherd. Then he said to his disciples, "The harvest is plentiful but the workers are few. Ask the Lord of the harvest, therefore, to send out workers into his harvest field."*
> (Matthew 9:36–38)

The message of the cross binds us together in a purposeful partnership. This is the good work that Jesus began on the cross. Before He ascended, Jesus told His disciples, "All authority in heaven and on earth has been given to me." Then He gave them a clear command: "Therefore go and make disciples of all nations." The *therefore* in His command is vital to understanding our job. Jesus is given all authority, *therefore*, under His authority and by His command we are to go and make disciples and baptize them in the name of the Father, Son, and Holy Spirit.

We are called to GO in Jesus' name, under His authority, and by His command. And all this is bound with prayers offered for every worker in the harvest field. This partnership is strengthened with prayer as we partner with Christ to complete the good work He began when He came to us as Immanuel, that is, God with us.

> *In all my prayers for all of you, I always pray with joy because of your partnership in the gospel from the first day until now, being confident of this, that he who began a good work in you will carry it on to completion until the day of Christ Jesus.*
> (Philippians 1:4–6)

When we do the work of the church, we need to be discipled and then sent into the harvest fields. Those who are sent need prayer warriors to cover them. Calling on the Lord with contrite hearts cleanses us and clears a path as we are sent out as ambassadors of Christ. The prayers of the saints shield workers in the harvest field from the enemy's fiery arrows. Intercessions of the church deliver God's servants from those who fiercely oppose the message of the gospel. Petitions sent up by partners in prayer strengthen and protect Jesus' disciples who proclaim the message of saving grace. When we lift church workers in prayer, their hearts abound in God's love and the Spirit's persevering strength as they are sent in Christ's name with power and authority to proclaim the Good News.

> As for other matters, brothers and sisters, pray for us that the message of the Lord may spread rapidly and be honored, just as it was with you. And pray that we may be delivered from wicked and evil people, for not everyone has faith. But the Lord is faithful, and he will strengthen you and protect you from the evil one. We have confidence in the Lord that you are doing and will continue to do the things we command. May the Lord direct your hearts into God's love and Christ's perseverance. (2 Thessalonians 3:1–5)

Chapter 1 Q&A

Pray for the Harvest

1. What are the essential elements of a successful harvest?

_____

_____

_____

2. Why are repentant prayers so vital as we prepare to work in the harvest fields?

_____

_____

_____

3. When we repent, is it only for our own sins? What about the sin that's all around us?

_____

_____

_____

4. Describe how a harvest worker is prepared and sent with the gospel to neighbors and nations.

_____

_____

_____

My Journey's Journal:

Chapter 2: The Joy of Harvesters

Key Scriptures:

- "For what is our hope, our joy, or the crown in which we will glory in the presence of our Lord Jesus when he comes? Is it not you? Indeed, you are our glory and joy" (1 Thessalonians 2:19–20).

- "Even now the one who reaps draws a wage and harvests a crop for eternal life, so that the sower and the reaper may be glad together" (John 4:36).

People in every borough have special ways to celebrate their harvests. Americans follow the tradition begun by the pilgrims who landed on New Plymouth's shores and expressed the joy of their first harvest by inviting their native tribesmen to a Thanksgiving feast. The Nguni people in Swaziland hold a ceremony with offerings of the first fruits of the harvest. Observant Israelis celebrate with a feast while living in makeshift huts during Sukkot, honoring God who assures regular weeks of harvest. Germans are well known for their Oktoberfests. When the harvest is finally gathered in, people can put their weariness and hunger behind them and celebrate.

But the joy of the harvest is even greater in the kingdom of heaven. God's people are called to do the work of the Great Commission by working in the harvest field. Then, when the work of harvesting souls for God's kingdom is at last complete, we find that the fruit of our labor is more than enough meat and drink to satisfy us. Those who began the field work, those who tend the fields, and workers who gather rejoice together.

A prayer according to Isaiah 9:3:

Oh, Lord of the harvest, enlarge your holy nation and increase our joy as you prepare our hearts for the harvest when we will enjoy its abundant fruits.

A runner who trains with ankle weights feels like he's running on air after he takes them off. Likewise, when the chains of sin are broken and the burdens of our past are lifted, we soar like the eagles. We carried the burdens of our past and bore sin's chains with tears, but our Redeemer sets us free and brings us into the joy of His salvation. The days of looking at our stumbling feet bogged down in sorrow are behind us. Our Savior lifts our heads like gates that open to the

King of glory.[1] Tears and sorrow are behind us, and we can return home with songs of rejoicing, carrying the fruit of a bountiful harvest.

> *Those who sow with tears will reap with songs of joy. Those who go out weeping, carrying seed to sow, will return with songs of joy, carrying sheaves with them.* (Psalm 126:5–6)

There is great joy in working together, each according to their spiritual gift. If we all had the same gift from the Holy Spirit, we would constantly till the soil with no one to sow the seed, tend the crop, or reap the harvest.[2] Each one does their part, and we all look forward to seeing the reapers finish the work so that everyone who worked in the fields profits from the harvest.

Jesus' Great Commission rallies us together to work as a team to complete the work of spreading the gospel message. Together we serve under His authority. We're compelled by His command to "go and make disciples," each one doing their job and working together like a family. All the people who serve among us have done their part, and we all rejoice together with an abundant harvest feast.

> *Thus the saying "One sows and another reaps" is true. I sent you to reap what you have not worked for. Others have done the hard work, and you have reaped the benefits of their labor.* (John 4:37–38)

After a long day on the job, the weariness of hard work turns into a good tired when we take a moment to give thanks for what the whole crew accomplished. When Barnabas arrived in Antioch, he marveled at the good work the grace of God had accomplished in the local church. Barnabas did his part in God's work among the believers in Antioch, and he was so delighted to see what others accomplished as faithful workers in the harvest field. Then he pressed on in the work among the saints by encouraging them to continue growing in grace and knowledge of Christ. But Barnabas couldn't do this work by himself. He went to find Paul to share in the church's work.

> *When he arrived and saw what the grace of God had done, he was glad and encouraged them all to remain true to the Lord with all their hearts.* (Acts 11:23)

Our natural tendency is to applaud our own efforts and expect accolades for the good things we achieved. But that attitude puts us on a perilous pedestal. A better way to accomplish the work of God's kingdom is to see ourselves as unworthy servants who have only done our duty.[3] We work together under Christ's authority as we "press on toward the goal to win the prize for which God has

---

1 Psalm 24:7–9.
2 Isaiah 28:24–26.
3 Luke 17:10.

called" us.[4] If we work in our own strength and by our own means, our work ends up as little more than straw that will not pass through the fire.[5]

When Jesus said, "they will do even greater things than these"[6] He meant the church joined as coworkers in making disciples who spread the gospel. Consider this example. If we tried to build a house on our own, cutting down our own trees to make lumber, making our own saws, hammers, nails, and hardware, we would fail miserably and wear ourselves out. The job of building God's kingdom is the work of servants who come together in Christ and serve by the empowering work of the Holy Spirit. When this happens, we'll return from the harvest fields singing songs of joy.

So neither the one who plants nor the one who waters is anything, but only God, who makes things grow. The one who plants and the one who waters have one purpose, and they will each be rewarded according to their own labor. For we are co-workers in God's service; you are God's field, God's building.
(1 Corinthians 3:7–9)

A teacher is blessed to see the outcome of her work when she bumps into her former students and sees that they're doing well. It's such a blessing to meet their happy, healthy children bundled up in the grocery cart. How much more blessed are God's servants who work in the harvest fields and bring lost souls into the blessed presence of Christ. These redeemed souls are cause for celebration because they are our joy and crown. Our hope is strengthened as we watch them grow in grace and knowledge and become faithful disciples who are called by God's holy name. We rejoice as we gather to worship, because these redeemed souls will sparkle like jewels in a crown.[7]

For what is our hope, our joy, or the crown in which we will glory in the presence of our Lord Jesus when he comes? Is it not you? Indeed, you are our glory and joy.
(1 Thessalonians 2:19–20)

We serve a God who is more than able to complete every good work He begins. He teaches the farmer how to work his land,[8] and in the same way He teaches us how to work in the harvest fields in His kingdom.

Consider God's faithfulness. He entreats us to pray for workers in the harvest field because the workers are few. Our heavenly Father raises up workers who must work together. One breaks up the fallow ground. He sends some to sow

---

4 Philippians 3:14.
5 1 Corinthians 3:13.
6 John 14:12.
7 Zechariah 9:16.
8 Isaiah 28:26.

good seed. He sends other workers to water the seed and still others to bring in the bounty. All workers serve with one purpose, and He rewards all according to their labor. Come, let's join in the harvest, each doing our part so we may come together in a great celebration.

> Then another angel came out of the temple and called in a loud voice to him who was sitting on the cloud, "Take your sickle and reap, because the time to reap has come, for the harvest of the earth is ripe." So he who was seated on the cloud swung his sickle over the earth, and the earth was harvested (Revelation 14:15–16).

Chapter 2 Q&A

The Joy of the Harvesters

1. Why are various spiritual gifts necessary to accomplish the work of the Great Commission?

_____

_____

_____

2. What is the result if people attempt to do the work of the church in their own strength and by their own abilities?

_____

_____

_____

3. Describe the joy of working together as we press on toward the goal to win the prize.

_____

_____

_____

My Journey's Journal:

Chapter 3: Count the Cost

Key Scriptures:

- "Anyone who loves their father or mother more than me is not worthy of me; anyone who loves their son or daughter more than me is not worthy of me" (Matthew 10:37).

- "If the world hates you, keep in mind that it hated me first. If you belonged to the world, it would love you as its own. As it is, you do not belong to the world, but I have chosen you out of the world. That is why the world hates you. Remember what I told you: 'A servant is not greater than his master.' If they persecuted me, they will persecute you also. If they obeyed my teaching, they will obey yours also. They will treat you this way because of my name, for they do not know the one who sent me" (John 15:18–21).

What does love cost you? Add up the numbers and you'll see that love costs you everything. Before you say your vows, it's good to consider the cost of becoming one, because you get married for better or worse. Love for your spouse and for your children compels you to give of yourself, even if it costs all that you have.

Salvation is a gift that is ours by faith alone. We're forgiven of so much, and this mercy is ours at a great cost—paid in full on our behalf. Our love of Christ, our Savior, compels us to follow Him as a disciple, knowing that it's costly to answer the call. The closer we follow, the greater the cost. If we are "all in" as ambassadors of Christ, it will cost us everything.

When ungodly people see Jesus manifested in our daily life, they often hate us even more. The greater the work the Holy Spirit accomplishes through us on behalf of God's kingdom, the more they'll despise us. Jesus has an answer for these sufferings; "I have told you these things, so that in me you may have peace. In this world you will have trouble. But take heart! I have overcome the world."[1]

A prayer according to Luke 14:27:

Heavenly Father, strengthen us by the power of your word and the Holy Spirit so we may bear our cross and serve faithfully as Jesus' disciples.

When you're recruiting volunteers, the first people to eagerly jump on board are often the first to give up when the going gets tough. They didn't count the

1 John 16:33.

cost of serving. Jesus showed us the way of the cross, and the apostle Paul teaches that benefits come with suffering.[2] Jesus never promised His followers an easy road—He promised trouble.[3] Those who are reluctant but take time o prayerfully consider what the job requires are the best and most resilient workers in the fields of harvest.

Jesus warns us against building a house without checking our savings account. If we don't, our half-finished house will be laughable.[4] People who count the cost to be sure of their resources before they build are the ones who finish the job and then enjoy the fruit of their labor.

> But don't begin until you count the cost. For who would begin construction of a building without first calculating the cost to see if there is enough money to finish it? Otherwise, you might complete only the foundation before running out of money, and then everyone would laugh at you. They would say, "There's the person who started that building and couldn't afford to finish it!"
> (Luke 14:28–30 (NLT)

When we step up to do the work God prepared in advance for us to do[5] we're not offered the keys to a fine home to rest and relax. We're not guaranteed paid time off as an incentive to start our job in God's kingdom. Instead, Jesus warns us not to look back at what we've left behind. He speaks of leaving our houses, brothers and sisters, father and mother, and the family farm for His sake. What He promises instead is a hundred times as much and an eternal inheritance.[6]

> As they were walking along the road, a man said to him,
> "I will follow you wherever you go."
> Jesus replied, "Foxes have dens and birds have nests, but the Son of Man has no place to lay his head."
> He said to another man, "Follow me."
> But he replied, "Lord, first let me go and bury my father."
> Jesus said to him, "Let the dead bury their own dead, but you go and proclaim the kingdom of God."
> Still another said, "I will follow you, Lord; but first let me go back and say goodbye to my family."
> Jesus replied, "No one who puts a hand to the plow and looks back is fit for service in the kingdom of God."
> (Luke 9:57–62)

After Jesus fed the five thousand, He had a large crowd pursuing Him. They wanted more free meals. "Sir," they said, "always give us this bread."[7] They were

---

2 Romans 5:3—5.
3 John 16:33.
4 Luke 14:28—30.
5 Ephesians 2:10.
6 Matthew 19:29.
7 John 6:34.

no better than their ancestors who demanded a king.[8] The people led by Israel's judges wanted a ruler who would provide for them and fight their battles. The crowd's purpose in seeking Jesus was not to serve Yahweh, their God, but to be served fresh bread and meat every day. Their stomach was their god,[9] and they wanted to force Jesus to serve as king for their belly's sake. But that's not the way of the kingdom of heaven.

> *Jesus, knowing that they intended to come and make him king by force, withdrew again to a mountain by himself.*
> (John 6:15)

When Jesus' disciples returned with food they bought in a Samaritan town, Jesus told them, "My food is to do the will of him who sent me and to finish His work."[10] The apostle Paul wrote to the Philippian church, thanking them for sharing in his troubles. He was content no matter his situation, "whether well fed or hungry, whether living in plenty or in want," Paul was always thankful.[11] The Holy Spirit told Ananias to warn Paul how much he would suffer for Christ's name.[12] Then Paul pressed on to serve zealously, and it cost him everything— he was stoned, run out of town, his life threatened many times, imprisoned in chains, and finally martyred for the cause of Christ. But serving Christ was of greater value to him than any of the world's comforts.

> *If anyone comes to me and does not hate father and mother, wife and children, brothers and sisters—yes, even their own life—such a person cannot be my disciple.*
> (Luke 14:26)

If it's your dream to restore an old car, don't start the job without preparing for what the job demands. First consider the busted knuckles, long hours, and the expense. If you don't, you may end up with a garage full of rusty car parts.

Jesus' followers must take an account of the cost of walking in His footsteps and suffering for the cross. When Jesus becomes Lord of our life, He disrupts our old self-serving lifestyle. If we don't consider the cost of giving that up, we may get discouraged and never accomplish our part in the work of the great commission. We'll end up trying to do a job we're not prepared to complete.

The world's torments and persecutions may alarm us and discourage our efforts. We must be strengthened to resist adversaries like Sanballat who fought against those who were digging through the wreckage and debris to rebuild Jerusalem.[13] The power of prayer and godly wisdom kept Nehemiah from burning out before the rebuilding was finished.[14]

8 1 Samuel 8:6.
9 Philippians 3:19.
10 John 6:23.
11 Philippians 4:12—13.
12 Acts 9:16.
13 Nehemiah 4:1—3.
14 Nehemiah 4:4—6.

And whoever does not carry their cross and follow me cannot be my disciple.
(Luke 14:27)

We serve a Savior who died a cruel death on a Roman cross. We walk in the footsteps of the apostles and prophets who laid the foundations for the church while suffering unimaginable persecutions. They were jeered, flogged, imprisoned in chains, stoned, sawn in two, and slain by the sword. Some of them wore sheepskins and goatskins for clothes. They were destitute and abused.[15]

But there is no reason to be ashamed of them because they carried the testimony of our resurrected Lord and Savior. They rejoiced to be counted worthy to join with Christ in His suffering to advance God's kingdom. Now we are called to walk on the pathway they blazed before us.

So do not be ashamed of the testimony about our Lord or of me his prisoner. Rather, join with me in suffering for the gospel, by the power of God.
(2 Timothy 1:8)

Lay all your stuff out on the kitchen table. Empty your pockets, pull out your credit cards, toss your bank statements on the pile, hand over your savings stash, and don't hold back your piggy bank. Pull your resume from the file, add your graduation certificate to the growing mound, and then put your trophies and awards with all the rest. Tally it all up and write down the numbers. This, and even more, is what it will cost you to go and work in the harvest fields in God's kingdom.

Prepare yourselves and count the cost so you may finish the good work you are called to accomplish in the fields of harvest. Then prepare yourself to celebrate a bountiful harvest with other faithful workers who have each done their part.

> Then Paul answered, "Why are you weeping and breaking my heart? I am ready not only to be bound, but also to die in Jerusalem for the name of the Lord Jesus."
> (Acts 21:13)

---

15 Hebrews 11:36—38.

Chapter 3 Q&A

Count the Cost

1. What is the first thing you must do before building a house for your family?

_____

_____

_____

2. How do we prepare for the Sanballat types who oppose us? Why is it important to be ready for them?

_____

_____

_____

3. What will you give up to follow Christ and raise His banner of love before the nations?

_____

_____

_____

4. What is our food while doing the work of our calling in Jesus Christ?

_____

_____

_____

My Journey's Journal:

Chapter 4: As the Father Sent Me

Key Scriptures:

- "'Peace be with you!' After he said this, he showed them his hands and side. The disciples were overjoyed when they saw the Lord. Again Jesus said, 'Peace be with you! As the Father has sent me, I am sending you.' And with that he breathed on them and said, 'Receive the Holy Spirit. If you forgive anyone's sins, their sins are forgiven; if you do not forgive them, they are not forgiven'" (John 20:19–23).

- "Then Jesus came to them and said, 'All authority in heaven and on earth has been given to me. Therefore go and make disciples of all nations, baptizing them in the name of the Father and of the Son and of the Holy Spirit, and teaching them to obey everything I have commanded you. And surely I am with you always, to the very end of the age'" (Matthew 28:18–20).

Whether we go to a neighbor or far-off nation to proclaim the Good News of forgiveness in Christ, we go with, in, under, and through the authority of Christ Jesus' holy name. Our Savior is Head of the church that disciples us before it sends us out as ambassadors of the cross. Then, guided by the Spirit of Christ, the elders lay hands to impart the Holy Spirit's empowering work that enables those they send to do the impossible work of God's eternal kingdom. By Jesus' command, He compels us to go in His name to do the good work God prepared in advance for each one of us to do.

Jesus sends us as His disciples with a message of forgiveness and saving grace. He sends us in the same way the Father sent Him—with the heart of a servant, in the power of the Spirit, and under authority. He sends us to proclaim peace and forgiveness for repentant sinners. Remember that Christ Jesus is given all authority in heaven and on earth and now He sends us as His ambassadors to proclaim His forgiveness to every nation on earth and serve as His hand extended to a world steeped in darkness.

A prayer according to John 14:12–14:

Spirit of Grace, open our eyes to see Christ in us so we may extend our hands to do what you are doing. Open our mouths to speak what you are speaking. Rally your church to do "greater things than these" in Jesus' holy name, for the honor and glory of the Father and Son.

If a married couple only focuses on looking good in front of family and friends, their relationship is on thin ice. If they won't do the hard work of building a strong relationship, a healthy family of faith, and a safe home, they build on sand.

In the same way, the church must not rely on external rituals and traditions.[1] Concentrating on calendars, council agendas, and programs to preserve religious practices and paradigms gets us nowhere. Instead, we are appointed to have the attitude of Christ. Then, by the authority of His command we can "go and make disciples." We are discipled and trained so we may do the work of the Great Commission. We are sent out as ambassadors of Christ in Jesus' holy name. In His name and by the power of His name, the whole church working together is empowered to do "greater things."[2]

All the people were amazed and said to each other, "What words these are! With authority and power he gives orders to impure spirits and they come out!"
(Luke 4:36)

Take nothing of your own with you as you go from town to town to minister. None of your natural abilities or personal strengths can accomplish the work God desires to carry out through you. Can you, by your own arguments, convince someone to become a Christian? Is it possible to persuade someone to be baptized using your personal charisma? Put these things aside and go out to speak, serve, and extend your hands by the empowering of the Holy Spirit and by the authority of Jesus' name. You have nothing of your own to offer wandering souls.

But Christ in you, the Word in you, and the Holy Spirit in you are powerfully effective in proclaiming forgiveness, healing, and eternal life.

"When you enter a town and are welcomed, eat what is offered to you. Heal the sick who are there and tell them, The kingdom of God has come near to you."
(Luke 10:8–9)

Raise Christ's banner so that all may see that He is the Son of the Living God who is mighty to save. Let us proclaim the Lord's life-giving death until He comes again.[3] When we declare Christ and His vicarious atonement, He draws lost and wandering souls.[4] When we go out with the light of Christ radiating from us, the truth of the gospel will challenge all those around us. It awakens them to the guilt of their sin. People are confronted with undeniable signs of Christ's living and active presence. Those who hear the gospel are convinced that Jesus is the Redeemer who saves. Those who encounter the truth and the

---

1 Old Testament worship and rites served as external signs that offered a covering for sin as they waited for the promised Messiah. Under the New Covenant the blood of Christ cleanses us from within—even our conscience. (Hebrews 9:13—14).

2 John 14:12—14.

3 1 Corinthians 11:26.

4 John 12:32.

reality of Christ will either scoff and be crushed by the Rock or broken with grief and come to repent of their sins.

When we see the powerful effect of God's Word, it gives us pause when we're about to speak our own words.

So Jesus said, "When you have lifted up the Son of Man, then you will know that I am he and that I do nothing on my own but speak just what the Father has taught me.
(John 8:28)

Christ gives His ambassadors a commission of peace. We're appointed as heralds of Christ so that we may bring peace into a world torn by chaos. He sends us into a perilous world to proclaim, "The kingdom of heaven has come near you." Jesus confers His divine power upon us to serve as ministers of His good will.[5]

This is a totally impossible job on our own. We need the Holy Spirit to indwell us, go before us, cover us, and serve as the wind that carries the Word we speak to change the hearts of lost souls. When we proclaim God's saving grace and mercies, those who hear will be forgiven, cleansed, and healed. But those who stop up their ears will not be forgiven.

Again Jesus said, "Peace be with you! As the Father has sent me, I am sending you." And with that he breathed on them and said, "Receive the Holy Spirit. If you forgive anyone's sins, their sins are forgiven; if you do not forgive them, they are not forgiven."
(John 20:21–23)

The Old Testament prophets served by the power of the Spirit who rested upon them. They prophesied the coming Messiah who would come among us to minister with an unlimited measure of the Holy Spirit.

After Jesus ascended to heaven, He appeared to Paul and sent him to proclaim Christ and the cross with a good measure of the blessings of Christ whose Spirit indwelled him. Now, the priesthood of believers includes all Christians, and we are called to "be filled to the measure of all the fullness of God" so we, the church, may minister and serve with an abundant portion of Christ's blessings. The power of the Spirit of Jesus sends us to proclaim the glad tidings of salvation through Christ and the promise of entering God's eternal rest. All followers of Christ are the church universal, and we are infused with a full measure of the blessings of the Spirit of Christ. We are sent just as the Father sent His Son, Jesus.

I know that when I come to you, I will come in the full measure of the blessing of Christ.
(Romans 15:29)

5 John 12:32.

The God of all creation sent His only Son as Immanuel, God with us. He came in humility as a servant. He walked among us to minister, and God gave Him the Spirit without limit.[6] Jesus came with the authority given to Him to do what He saw the Father doing. He reached out His hand to those the Father touched and to speak what the Father spoke.

Now, our Lord Jesus sends us in the same way to proclaim His forgiveness to the people of every nation. With His command, under His authority, and speaking what the Spirit speaks[7] we humbly and powerfully minister the Word with authority, walking in Jesus' footsteps.

If we are sent in our own strength, we build on shifting sand. Constructing our own house is like building with straw. Instead, we build on a solid foundation who is Jesus Christ. He sends us under the authority of His name to proclaim forgiveness and peace to all who will hear, believe, and receive the message of Good News. We give witness to what God has accomplished in us to neighbors and nations so they too may build upon the Rock.

> For this reason I kneel before the Father, from whom every family in heaven and on earth derives its name. I pray that out of his glorious riches he may strengthen you with power through his Spirit in your inner being, so that Christ may dwell in your hearts through faith. And I pray that you, being rooted and established in love, may have power, together with all the Lord's holy people, to grasp how wide and long and high and deep is the love of Christ, and to know this love that surpasses knowledge— that you may be filled to the measure of all the fullness of God. (Ephesians 3:14–19)

6 John 23:34.
7 Acts 6:10.

Chapter 4 Q&A

As the Father Sent Me

1. How did the Father send His Son to minister and serve among us?

_____

_____

_____

2. Why is it important to know how the Father sent Jesus?

_____

_____

_____

3. What should we take with us when we are sent as ambassadors of the cross?

_____

_____

_____

4. Describe the difference between an Old Testament prophet's ministry and the work of New Testament's priesthood of all believers.

_____

_____

_____

My Journey's Journal:

Chapter 5:
The Father, Son, and Holy Spirit Work Salvation

Key Scriptures:

- "For he chose us in him before the creation of the world to be holy and blameless in his sight. In love he predestined us for adoption to sonship through Jesus Christ, in accordance with his pleasure and will—to the praise of his glorious grace, which he has freely given us in the One he loves" (Ephesians 1:4–6).

- "In him we have redemption through his blood, the forgiveness of sins, in accordance with the riches of God's grace that he lavished on us. With all wisdom and understanding, he made known to us the mystery of his will according to his good pleasure, which he purposed in Christ, to be put into effect when the times reach their fulfillment—to bring unity to all things in heaven and on earth under Christ. In him we were also chosen, having been predestined according to the plan of him who works out everything in conformity with the purpose of his will, in order that we, who were the first to put our hope in Christ, might be for the praise of his glory. And you also were included in Christ when you heard the message of truth, the gospel of your salvation. When you believed, you were marked in him with a seal, the promised Holy Spirit, who is a deposit guaranteeing our inheritance until the redemption of those who are God's possession—to the praise of his glory" (Ephesians 1:7–14).

The writer of Ecclesiastes book of wisdom penned a great truth. "Though one may be overpowered, two can defend themselves. A cord of three strands is not quickly broken."[1] How does this truth apply to us today? When God's sons and daughters are woven into the three-stranded cord with our Lord and Savior Jesus Christ, the Father who loves us, and the fellowship of the Holy Spirit, we are made part of an unbreakable bond.

Before the Creator began the work of creation, He chose all His sons and daughters whom He would call by His holy name. Before the universe's clock started marking time, He chose a family to be redeemed through the blood sacrifice of His one and only Son, Jesus Christ. All those who hear and believe that

---

1 Ecclesiastes 4:12.

Jesus is the Christ are marked with a Trinitarian guarantee of an eternal inheritance. Now we are called to proclaim this great salvation to the nations, baptize them into the name of the Father, Son, and Holy Spirit, and make them disciples of Christ.

> A prayer according to Hebrews 6:13 and 2 Corinthians 1:20–22:
>
> Oh, God of our great promise, bring us into your covenant of grace through your Son and the Spirit of Grace who deposits the AMEN of our faith within us.

The Father

From the beginning to the end of all time, our heavenly Father tenders His saving grace to those He adopts as sons and daughters. Before the first day of creation and before God set the foundations of the earth in place, He loved us as His children and prepared a way to make us holy and blameless children of resurrection.[2] Our Lord and God watches over us to redeem us.[3] He knew us before the moment we were conceived. He leads us to hear His message of peace proclaimed so that the seed of faith is planted in our hearts. Then He feeds us on His Word so we may grow in grace and knowledge. He holds us in the hallow of His hands until the day we are united with our Savior in a resurrection like His.[4]

Praise be to the God and Father of our Lord Jesus Christ, who has blessed us in the heavenly realms with every spiritual blessing in Christ. For he chose us in him before the creation of the world to be holy and blameless in his sight. In love he predestined us for adoption to sonship through Jesus Christ, in accordance with his pleasure and will–to the praise of his glorious grace, which he has freely given us in the One he loves.
(Ephesians 1:3–6)

Before time began, the Creator chose us as the children He would gather as His holy nation.[5] He chose us before we did anything good or bad.[6] Then, when our loving heavenly Father knit us together in our mother's womb, He formed and shaped every element of our being.[7] He knows our hearts, attitudes, thoughts, and every word we speak even before we say them. He knows our career choices before we do. We chose a place to live on planet earth, but God watches over us, already knowing where to find us.

Who have been chosen according to the foreknowledge of God the Father, through the sanctifying work of the Spirit, to be obedient to Jesus Christ and sprinkled with his blood:

---

2 Luke 20:36.
3 Psalm 121:5—8.
4 Romans 6:5.
5 1 Peter 2:9.
6 2 Timothy 1:9.
7 Psalm 139:13.

28

Grace and peace be yours in abundance.
(1 Peter 1:2)

The Son

Since the beginning of all the heavens and earth, the Word of creation revealed the Father's invisible qualities, eternal power, and divine nature.[8] He continues to hold all of creation together by His word.[9] Those powerful and creative words, "Let there be light," set in place the foundations for all that He created. From the beginning He established forgiveness and saving grace for those created in God's likeness.

Then He came at the right time to fulfill the Mosaic law just as all the Old Testament prophets had proclaimed. He came as Immanuel, God with us, and provided a way of redemption by paying the sin debt in full for the whole world.

Before time began, the Word of creation knew our names, our life's purpose, and prepared the way for us to have fellowship our heavenly Father. God's Son made a way for us to be united with Himself and the indwelling Holy Spirit. He also prepared a job ahead of time for each of us to accomplish to advance His kingdom.[10]

In him we have redemption through his blood, the forgiveness of sins, in accordance with the riches of God's grace that he lavished on us. With all wisdom and understanding, he made known to us the mystery of his will according to his good pleasure, which he purposed in Christ, to be put into effect when the times reach their fulfillment—to bring unity to all things in heaven and on earth under Christ. In him we were also chosen, having been predestined according to the plan of him who works out everything in conformity with the purpose of his will, in order that we, who were the first to put our hope in Christ, might be for the praise of his glory.
(Ephesians 1:7–12)

Our Redeemer didn't come in a royal chariot sparkling with gold and jewels. He did not arrive dressed in royal splendor. Israel's teachers of the Law expected the Messiah to come as a lion, but He came as a lamb. He humbled Himself, and "made Himself nothing by taking on the very nature of a servant, being made in human likeness."[11] Jesus came in a way that reveals the true nature of God.

Consider what our Savior has done for us. If our hands overflowed with earth's treasures, our hands would still be empty of anything of eternal value. But those who are redeemed by the shed blood of our Savior, Jesus Christ, have a treasure stored up that cannot be corrupted by moths, rust, or pests. In Christ we have treasure in heaven that no thief can steal.[12]

8 Romans 1:20.
9 Colossians 1:17.
10 Ephesians 2:10.
11 Philippians 2:6—7.
12 Matthew 6:20.

For you know that it was not with perishable things such as silver or gold that you were redeemed from the empty way of life handed down to you from your ancestors, but with the precious blood of Christ, a lamb without blemish or defect.
(1 Peter 1:18–19)

Holy Spirit

The Word proclaims the saving grace of our God and Father, and this message is quickened in our heart by the Spirit of Jesus. The Holy Spirit pierces our hearts with redemptive truth of God's Word. When the gospel message is heard the Spirit of Christ plants the seed of faith in the hearts of those who are called and chosen.[13] He convinces us of our sin, convicts us of our sin, and brings our hearts to repentance. He cleanses repentant hearts, minds, and consciences, working from the inside out.[14] The Spirit of Jesus gives us the gift of saving faith so that we may believe in Jesus as our Savior who died in our place and for our sins, was buried, rose up victorious from the grave, and ascended to the right hand of the Father where He intercedes on our behalf.

The Spirit of grace seals us against God's just and righteous wrath. He indwells, encompasses, and covers us with His holy presence in every moment of the day and night. He helps us pray and interprets our prayers,[15] presenting our petitions before the throne of grace, even with groaning on our behalf. He encompasses us every step along the way as the Spirit of counsel and of power, the Spirit of knowledge and the fear of the Lord, so that we may delight in the fear of the Lord.[16]

And you also were included in Christ when you heard the message of truth, the gospel of your salvation. When you believed, you were marked in him with a seal, the promised Holy Spirit, who is a deposit guaranteeing our inheritance until the redemption of those who are God's possession—to the praise of his glory.
(Ephesians 1:13–14)

The Spirit of life accomplishes a good work in all God's sons and daughters. He plants the seed of faith in our hearts, breathes new life into us, washes and cleanses us, seals us, and then gifts and empowers us for a good work in His kingdom. The Spirit of wisdom and knowledge keeps us walking in the light and continually cleanses us from all sin by the blood of Jesus.[17] The Spirit of Jesus creates a clean heart in us to keep us steadfast in our faith.[18] Through the Eternal Spirit, Jesus offered Himself without blemish as an acceptable sacrifice that cleanses our consciences.[19] He keeps us in sweet fellowship, lighting our pathway. The Spirit of

13 Romans 10:17.
14 Hebrews 10:22.
15 Romans 8:26—27.
16 Isaiah 11:2—3.
17 1 John 1:7.
18 Psalm 51:10.
19 Hebrews 9:14.

30

Christ warns us away from unrighteous acts against God, so we may enter God's eternal rest.

> *And do not grieve the Holy Spirit of God, with whom you were sealed for the day*
> *of redemption.*
> (Ephesians 4:30)

From the beginning of time, the Creator knew everything about you. Before you had a chance to do anything right or wrong, He chose you to be His son or daughter, called by His holy name. Then, from the moment you were born, the Triune God triple teamed you to bring you before the throne of grace with a repentant heart. By this great love and saving grace you are interwoven with this three-stranded, unbreakable cord that secures you on the path of faith. This awesome work of redemption is yours by means of the Father, Son, and Holy Spirit.

Yet to all who did receive him, to those who believed in his name, he gave the right to become children of God—children born not of natural descent, nor of human decision or a husband's will, but born of God. The Word became flesh and made his dwelling among us. We have seen his glory, the glory of the one and only Son, who came from the Father, full of grace and truth. (John 1:12–14)

Chapter 5 Q&A

The Father, Son, and Holy Spirit Work Salvation

1. When did your heavenly Father choose you as His own?

_____

_____

_____

2. Why is it so comforting that salvation is the work of a Triune God?

_____

_____

_____

3. Is believing that Jesus came in the flesh to redeem us vital to our faith?

_____

_____

_____

4. What is the Holy Spirit's part in the work that brings us to God's saving grace?

_____

_____

_____

My Journey's Journal:

Part II
Emptied of its Power

"To preach the gospel—not with wisdom and eloquence, lest the cross of Christ be emptied of its power."
(1 Corinthians 1:17)

Jesus said, "Follow me and I will make you fishers of men."[1] But what do we do after we catch them? This part of our learning quest alerts us to the church's responsibilities and some of the hazards we encounter as we go fishing.

---

1 Matthew 4:19.

Chapter 6: Catch and Release

Key Scriptures:

- "Come, follow me," Jesus said, "and I will send you out to fish for people" (Matthew 4:19).

- "Those who are wise will shine like the brightness of the heavens, and those who lead many to righteousness, like the stars for ever and ever" (Daniel 12:3).

The best day of fishing is when you do a lot of catching. It's a bit painful to have to throw that beautiful rainbow trout back in the lake after you net it and remove the hook. Those who fish for lost souls catch and rejoice. They don't throw them back in the river. Sending them into the deep to sink or swim on their own is not God's plan. We can't injure them with God's commands, see them redeemed through the gospel of Jesus Christ, and then toss them back in the murky waters of this sin-stained world.

When we proclaim Christ as Lord and Savior, this affects every aspect of a person's life. We hold out God's abundant forgiveness to them. The Savior extends mercy and compels them to love Him and obey all that He has commanded us. When redeemed souls are brought to saving faith and baptized, this is just a good beginning. We guide and train God's newborn sons and daughters to follow Christ Jesus as Lord, with the Word as their light and the Holy Spirit as their guide.

A prayer according to Ephesians 4:11–13:

Oh, Christ Jesus, Head of the church, equip your people to do the work of your kingdom so that the body of Christ may be built up in the unity of the faith and full knowledge of our Lord and Savior.

Few modern-day people know the meaning and significance of "lord" or "lordship" in the Scriptures. We're very uninformed about the historic biblical meaning of "kings" and "kingdoms." Post-modern Christians are often ill-informed about what it means to submit to Christ's authority. All we know about lordship is that when the landlord knocks on our door, we need to pay our rent and the house better not be a wreck.

What does it mean to serve Christ as Lord? When we answer our Savior's call and come to saving faith, Jesus desires to be more than a ticket to heaven. He teaches us to make Him Lord of our lives. Why would anyone want a Savior who is not Lord of their everyday lives?

Those who refuse Him as Lord fall short of God's promised rest.[1] He yearns for us to live as Jesus instructed us so we may walk according to the Spirit.[2] His desire is for the Spirit of Christ to guide us into all truth so we may live in agreement with righteousness and speak what is right and true.[3]

When Jesus is our Lord, we cannot compartmentalize our lives into a church life and an everyday life. They are intricately intertwined. We can't swim in calm, clear Christian Lake on Sunday and then paddle on our own in the turbulent tide waters of Deception Pass the rest of the week.[4]

So then, just as you received Christ Jesus as Lord, continue to live your lives in him, rooted and built up in him, strengthened in the faith as you were taught, and overflowing with thankfulness.
(Colossians 2:6–7)

We are called to live as children of the light. Children of hope have attitudes of loving servants who look to the hand of their merciful master.[5] Our heart's desire is to please our Lord Jesus Christ. We search the Scriptures to know what He desires of us. We're thirsty to hear Spirit inspired teachers who help us learn the gospel's commands. Children of resurrection get hungry and listen to anointed preachers who speak out to instruct us in the way we should go so we may walk in the light of Christ. This is important because those who are baptized but not taught to become disciples may soon die out like seeds that sprout in rocky soil.[6]

For you were once darkness, but now you are light in the Lord. Live as children of light.
(Ephesians 5:8)

Christians may be too impetuous in our efforts to convert people who will then come to our church. We compel them to answer an altar call, lead them to repeat a prayer, or have them fill out a commitment card with their name and contact information, and then check the "New Believer" and "I want to be baptized" boxes. We're so anxious to add to our church statistics that we turn conversion of lost souls into a transaction. Our evangelistic methods become external and dispirited. We end up with a church filled with people who call themselves Christians but have no hunger or thirst for righteousness.

---

1 Hebrews 4:1—2.
2 Galatians 5:25.
3 John 16:13.
4 A reference to the raging tide water of Deception Pass near Oak Harbor, Washington.
5 Psalm 123:2.
6 Matthew 13:5.

When the gospel message cuts to the heart, this compels people to plead, "What must I do?" The Holy Spirit plants the seed of faith in their hearts by hearing the Word. They're called and chosen to be adopted as God's sons and daughters. We give them a clear and simple answer: "Come to the water and the Word, and be baptized into the name of the Father, Son, and Holy Spirit."

Those who are born from above become new creations in Christ. A new believer is God's handiwork. A reborn person is created to do good works prepared in advance for them. Those who come to saving faith need to be discipled to deny themselves and take up their cross to follow in Jesus' footsteps.

Redeemed souls are like clay in the potter's hands, and it's mighty uncomfortable getting reshaped. We must disciple them in the Holy Spirit's comfort. They must know that when Christ Jesus becomes Lord and Master of their lives, He leads them out of their old lifestyle. The best evangelism efforts proclaim a clear and simple gospel and then teach new believers to run free on Jesus' narrow pathway. Fully committed worshippers will then fill our gatherings. We are called to make disciples whom Christ has called to His saving grace so they may love, obey, and serve Jesus as Lord.

And so it was with me, brothers and sisters. When I came to you, I did not come with eloquence or human wisdom as I proclaimed to you the testimony about God. (1 Corinthians 2:1)

When a new believer is baptized, they are called to remain in their baptism. That is, to continue in Christ and live in agreement with the washing of water and the Word. God loved us first so that now we can love Him.[7] Jesus instructs His followers, "If you love me, keep my commands."[8] Love and obedience go together like morning and a sunrise. A newborn Christian's faith and love of Christ compels them to learn how to obey what Jesus desires of them.

But we must be clear about good deeds. What we do to please God does not make us righteous. Righteousness from God comes only by faith in Jesus Christ.[9]

A new believer's heart overflows with joy because of Christ's love. But this is just a good beginning of a life filled with rejoicing. Their joy is incomplete if they do not remain in His love, abide in Christ, and keep His commandments. But if we are taught to exalt baptism as our hope and security rather than the name we're baptized into, our baptism is only external—by the hands of man.

Genuine confidence is ours because we are baptized into the name of the Father, Son, and Holy Spirit as our haven of rest. When we believe and are baptized, God leads us beside still waters and restores our wounded soul. We must not release new Christians with false promises or assumed security that leaves

---

7 John 4:19.
8 John 14:15.
9 Romans 3:22.

them to sink or swim in life's roiling storms.

> *As the Father has loved me, so have I loved you. Now remain in my love. If you keep my commands, you will remain in my love, just as I have kept my Father's commands and remain in his love. I have told you this so that my joy may be in you and that your joy may be complete.*
> (John 15:9–11)

The lordship of our Savior is a position of glory and majesty. Our Lord Jesus Christ is embued with authority and power as our High Priest. He is due all honor and respect, for He is Lord over all creation. Our Redeemer is exalted as Master and Messiah. He is worthy of all glory, awe, and praise. Our Lord and Savior commanded, and all things were created.[10] He is the One whom we serve as Lord. It's our job to school the fish we catch so they too may lift our Savior's banner to the nations.

Christ is the One who is mighty to save.[11] We serve an awesome God who is King above all kings and Lord above all lords. His desire is to be Lord of every part of a new believer's life. Our job as servants of Christ is to disciple them in paths of righteousness. We don't just send them on their way and hope they'll be okay.

> *For what we preach is not ourselves, but Jesus Christ as Lord, and ourselves as your servants for Jesus' sake.*
> (2 Corinthians 4:5)

If we send converts out before they are discipled, they don't learn that Jesus Christ also wants to be Lord of their lives. They'll swim in calm waters with other people of faith on Sunday and then splash like crazy to survive the stormy waters of life so they can gather with us again to get back a little peace. When left on their own, they end up no better off than the Israelites who had no king, not even God.

Those we send out to carry the vessels of the Lord must be cleansed, discipled, and taught to serve well. They are called to obey the gospel, imitate Christ, deny themselves, and depart from all that is unclean[12] so they may serve as "fishers of men."[13]

---

10 Psalm 148:5.
11 Isaiah 63:1.
12 Isaiah 52:11.
13 Matthew 4:19.

> When you heard about Christ and were taught in him in accordance with the truth that is in Jesus. You were taught, with regard to your former way of life, to put off your old self, which is being corrupted by its deceitful desires; to be made new in the attitude of your minds; and to put on the new self, created to be like God in true righteousness and holiness. (Ephesians 4:20–25)

Chapter 6 Q&A

Catch and Release

1. What does it mean to serve Christ as Lord of your life?

_____

_____

_____

2. If good deeds neither save nor obtain righteousness for us, why should we obey?

_____

_____

_____

3. Why does your lifestyle matter after you are brought to saving faith?

_____

_____

_____

4. What is the connection between love and obedience?

_____

_____

_____

5. What part of your life needs to be submitted to Christ as Lord?

_____

_____

_____

My Journey's Journal:

Chapter 7: Do Not Sow Among Thorns

Key Scriptures:

- "This is what the Lord says to the people of Judah and to Jerusalem: 'Break up your unplowed ground and do not sow among thorns'" (Jeremiah 4:3).

- "Do not give dogs what is sacred; do not throw your pearls to pigs. If you do, they may trample them under their feet, and turn and tear you to pieces" (Matthew 7:6)

When you're ready to plant your garden in the spring, the weeds and winter kill can be overwhelming. You waste your good seed if you just broadcast it among the thorns. Soil that is not broken up is too hard and unreceptive to new seeds and seedlings.

Fallow, weed-infested ground quickly chokes out seeds after they sprout. In the same way, the seed of God's Word cannot take root and grow in hard hearts. Unhearing souls are like fallow ground. If the ground is not properly prepared, the seeds of God's Word lie on top of the ground where the birds come to eat them.[1] When hardened hearts refuse to hear the gospel preached, they reject words of life. They'll oppose you and turn what you say against you. You cannot offer the gospel's forgiveness and comforts to people who continuously scorn God's grace and mercies. If you let them grow in your garden, they'll bring you to ruin.[2]

> A prayer according to Matthew 13:23:
>
> Oh, Lord of the harvest, strengthen us to sow the good seed of your word among those who hear, understand, believe, receive, and then produce and abundant crop.

We cannot offer solace to those who parade their unrepentant pride.[3] We must not affirm those who are rebellious, arrogant, or impenitent. When intransigent people are shown grace, they don't learn righteousness. Hearing the gospel hardens their hearts, and they go on doing evil.[4] It's counterproductive to offer support to people who hide their sin in servile fear of the Lord and shrink back from the splendor of His majesty.[5] People are left desolate if they plug their ears and stubbornly turn their

---

1 Matthew 13:4.
2 Nehemiah 13:6—9.
3 Isaiah 2:9.
4 Isaiah 26:10.
5 Isaiah 2:10.

backs, offended by the Good News.[6] Those who spurn the gospel's call stumble on the Rock and get trapped in a snare. When defiant souls hear the Good News, their hearts defy the truth. They trip up and get caught in the trap of their rebellion.[7]

What must we do when confronted by intractable people? Do we frighten them out of their sinful ways with threats of hell fire? Do we argue them out of their fears and ignorance? What can we do if they spit in our face when we witness to them?

Frightening, threatening, and arguing tactics never work. Instead, we turn the other cheek against persecution by revealing Christ—loving our enemies and blessing those who persecute us.[8] We must not give comfort while people persist in rebellion. But we can continue to proclaim the gospel message to them by showing the love, forgiveness, and the mercies of Christ who is ever present in our daily lives.

> To whom can I speak and give warning? Who will listen to me? Their ears are closed so they cannot hear. The word of the Lord is offensive to them; they find no pleasure in it.
> (Jeremiah 6:10)

Those who offer a show of holiness and false piety are the same ones who polish the outside of the cup and forget to clean out the greedy crud and the spoiling remnants of their self-indulgence on the inside.[9] They're like a person who hides a serious virus infection and goes around spreading the germs to everyone they meet. When they hear of Jesus, the remedy, they're offended. It hurts their feelings if you speak the truth in love.

Self-righteous people mask their duplicity with external ritualistic spiritual traditions. Everything they do looks good, sounds right, and makes a good show of religious sentiments. But it's a thin veneer. Don't get drawn in with them or they'll make you twice the children of hell that they are.[10]

> "Woe to you, because you are like unmarked graves, which people walk over without knowing it." One of the experts in the law answered him, "Teacher, when you say these things, you insult us also."
> (Luke 11:44–45)

Jesus spoke healing words filled with forgiveness, mercy, and saving grace. He offered a promise of eternal life. He walked among His own people as the light of the world.[11] But the religious stalwarts of the day rejected His words and accused

---

6 Zechariah 7:11—14.
7 Isaiah 8:14—15.
8 Romans 12:14.
9 Luke 11:39.
10 Matthew 23:15.
11 John 8:12.

Him of getting His power from the "ruler of demons."[12] They did their best to trap Jesus with His own words. But they couldn't because He spoke only what He heard the Father speaking[13] and could not be ensnared by their duplicity.

Jesus didn't speak words of mercy and forgiveness to these hard-hearted Pharisees and teachers of the law unless they repented. No, he spoke seven woes to them to warn them of God's wrath to come.[14] He spoke to the crowds in parables because they were "ever seeing but never perceiving, and ever hearing but never understanding."[15]

When Jesus went outside, the Pharisees and the teachers of the law began to oppose him fiercely and to besiege him with questions, waiting to catch him in something he might say.
(Luke 11:53–54)

Every garden needs a springtime cleanup. We must turn the soil and prepare it for seed. You can't plow a garden one year and never again if you expect a good crop next harvest season. Even good soil turns hard if it's not plowed by a diligent farmer. It's much the same in every Christian's walk of faith. We need to constantly hear the Word and listen to the convicting nudges of the Holy Spirit to keep our faith from wavering.

Those who share in Christ are called to gather so we may encourage and strengthen each other in our walk of faith. We need to stand together to keep our hearts from becoming hard. It's important to shield ourselves from the lifestyle of those who defiantly persist in the ways of the world and forsake the fellowship of believers.

See to it, brothers and sisters, that none of you has a sinful, unbelieving heart that turns away from the living God. But encourage one another daily, as long as it is called "Today," so that none of you may be hardened by sin's deceitfulness. We have come to share in Christ, if indeed we hold our original conviction firmly to the very end. As has just been said: "Today, if you hear his voice, do not harden your hearts as you did in the rebellion."
(Hebrews 3:12–15)

Imagine an inmate who gets used to gulping prison swill twice a day for many years. Finally, he is pardoned and goes home where Mom prepares ham and eggs for breakfast, BLT sandwiches for lunch, and cheese-smothered ravioli for dinner. Why would he ever want to go back and eat jailhouse stew again?

Those who the Spirit leads to the knowledge of Christ and His saving grace are sealed by the Holy Spirit for the day of redemption.[16] Then we must answer

12 Matthew 12:24.
13 John 12:49.
14 Matthew 13:23—39.
15 Mark 4:12.
16 Ephesians 4:30.

the call to bear our cross and "share abundantly in the sufferings of Christ."[17] This is possible because Jesus comforts us in our sufferings.

Why would we ever go back to be bound in the chains of sin? We must not allow ourselves to be dragged down by those who turn away after knowing the way of the cross. Grief overwhelms us as they turn from Christ because, "It is impossible for those who have once been enlightened, who have tasted the heavenly gift, who have shared in the Holy Spirit, who have tasted the goodness of the word of God and the powers of the coming age and who have fallen away, to be brought back to repentance."[18]

It would have been better for them not to have known the way of righteousness, than to have known it and then to turn their backs on the sacred command that was passed on to them. Of them the proverbs are true: "A dog returns to its vomit," and, "A sow that is washed returns to her wallowing in the mud."
(2 Peter 2:21–22)

If you want your message to get through, don't send it in the hands of a fool.[19] The greatest message ever heard is best entrusted to those who are tested and proven trustworthy as ambassadors.[20] They're strong and confident in the Lord. They don't shy away from admonishing those who are contradictory and just want to argue.

Those who are new to the faith can get confused by winds of doctrine. They may succumb to a shrewd and devious theology because of their lack of knowledge. New Christians need to mature in the faith to become reliable messengers of Christ and the cross. We entrust the Good News gospel message to those who will speak the truth in love and lead God's people to grow in grace and knowledge and honor Christ who is Head of the church.[21]

And the things you have heard me say in the presence of many witnesses entrust to reliable people who will also be qualified to teach others.
(2 Timothy 2:2)

When gardeners see something growing that they didn't plant, it's a weed. Invasive plants get yanked out and thrown in the burn pile. But thorns can get sneaky and grow hidden among the daisies. There are also wild sprouts that look like real flowers while they take over your garden.

The truth is that every plant our heavenly Father has not planted—religious opinions, superstitious practices, and prideful formalities—have no place in the garden of God. There is no room in the church for man-made ways of worship. Yet, we're all tempted to turn away, go rogue, and become wild olive branches.[22]

---

17 2 Corinthians 1:5.
18 Hebrews 6:4—6.
19 Proverbs 26:6.
20 Titus 1:9.
21 Ephesians 4:14—15.
22 Romans 11:17—24.

When invasive plants prosper among us, they squeeze out the seeds of the gospel that we sow. The thorns tend to blind us to the truth and distract us from proclaiming the truth so others to see the light of Christ.

> *He replied, "Every plant that my heavenly Father has not planted will be pulled up by the roots. Leave them; they are blind guides. If the blind lead the blind, both will fall into a pit."*
> (Matthew 15:13–14)

Jesus sent out His twelve disciples and seventy-two appointed followers to proclaim the peace of God's kingdom. They prepared the unplowed ground by preaching Good News to spiritually impoverished souls. Jesus' followers spread the seed of God's Word everywhere they went without discriminating. But Jesus gave them instructions. "If anyone will not welcome you or listen to your words, leave that home or town and shake the dust off your feet."[23]

He assured them that when they proclaimed the gospel's message of peace, it would rest on the peaceful. But where the people rejected God's peace, it would return to them. Jesus made it clear that when they wiped dust off their feet from towns that turned their backs on Christ, it would serve as a warning against them. They must leave and not labor in vain, not sowing more good seed among the thorns.

> Though on the day you set them out, you make them grow, and on the morning when you plant them, you bring them to bud, yet the harvest will be as nothing.
> (Isaiah 17:11)

---

23 Matthew 10:14, Luke 10:11.

Chapter 7 Q&A

Do Not Sow Among Thorns

1. What do you do to prepare your garden in the spring before you sow your tomato seeds?

_____

_____

_____

2. When we're sowing the seeds of God's Word, how do we respond to the people who are impenitent and rebellious?

_____

_____

_____

3. How did Jesus reply to the teachers of the Law who rejected His teaching?

_____

_____

_____

4. Describe the many "weeds" in the garden.
   What dangers do they pose for the church?

_____

_____

_____

My Journey's Journal:

Chapter 8: A Bandage for Their Wounds

Key Scriptures:

- "They dress the wound of my people as though it were not serious. 'Peace, peace,' they say, when there is no peace" (Jeremiah 8:11).

- "See to it that no one takes you captive through hollow and deceptive philosophy, which depends on human tradition and the elemental spiritual forces of this world rather than on Christ" (Colossians 2:8).

A suture can't fix a shattered bone. First-aid cream doesn't cure cancer. But we serve a God who provides a true remedy for sin's wounds. He sent His only Son, our Lord and Savior, who gave His body to be broken so that we may be healed in body, soul, and spirit. The blood of Jesus Christ offers forgiveness and cleanses the whole person of sin's stain so we may be completely restored. A Savior who was pierced is the cure.[1]

The church must not offer anything less than the fullness of Christ. The job of the church and its ministries is to restore people to wholeness in Christ. Our Redeemer's desire is to affect every aspect of our lives. His blood cleanses away bitterness and anger. He restores health, heals deep-felt wounds, renews our minds, changes attitudes, gives us a new worldview, and fills our hearts with the love of Christ.

A bandage gospel may offer a temporary cover but won't heal the conscience. No patch can heal from within. In the same way, a false gospel with pacifying promises can only tickle our ears with empty assurances and feel-good traditions. These things are straw.[2] They have little to do with Christ.

God's sons and daughters must know the true gospel message so well that any false hope or promise offered can be readily recognized and rejected.

A Prayer according to Isaiah 53:5:

Oh, Father of lights, reveal Christ to us so we may see and believe in our Savior who was pierced for our transgressions, crushed for our iniquities, and paid the penalty for our sins so that we may have peace with God and healing for our wounds.

---

1 Isaiah 53:5, 1 Peter 2:24.
2 1 Corinthians 3:12—15.

"I go to church to sing, pray and listen to the sermons. I was baptized and I pray every chance I get. I read Bible verse cards that I keep in my desk for when I'm on hold. So, I'm good to go to heaven, right? I have a good job and drive a new SUV. I play with my kids. They do great in school, and they enjoy Sunday school. My wife and I are happy together. We regularly donate to charity. Life is good. What can go wrong?"

Pure doctrine offers no benefit unless it causes us to pursue Christ and walk as He walked. Christian creeds are of little use if they don't inspire good deeds from the heart. Memorizing Scripture offers few benefits if we don't apply the words to our lives. What good is an offer of forgiveness if our hearts are unrepentant and we refuse to turn from our sins? If we hear God's Word but don't do it, we deceive ourselves.[3]

Many Christians claim pure doctrine, creeds of the church, memorizing verses, altars of repentance, baptism, and Scriptures about forgiveness to assure themselves that they will never be shaken. But love without obedience is a very thin veneer? Worshipping with a divided heart is like chaff that blows away in the wind.

He says to himself, "Nothing will ever shake me." He swears, "No one will ever do me harm."
(Psalm 10:6)

The prophet Jeremiah's oracles are still relevant. As he speaks, we can hear God's heart breaking over the wounds of His people who were crushed by idolatry. Their idols were an offense to the holy name of a righteous God. The stone images they set up on their high places had eyes but couldn't see. The cold, hard, golden idols had ears, but couldn't hear. The wooden carvings they worshipped led them into a covenant with death, a lie that offered no refuge.[4] Chiseled stone images were no more than decorations that offered false promises and empty hopes.

The wounds of sin among God's people were serious and malignant. Israel turned a deaf ear to Yahweh who had delivered them from slavery. They shunned His loving commands. Their hearts had turned away from God who heals.[5] Instead, they preferred to cover up their injuries with false hopes.

Is there no balm in Gilead? Is there no physician there? Why then is there no healing for the wound of my people?
(Jeremiah 8:22)

Denying ourselves and taking up our cross is a hard teaching to accept. It's against our human nature to give up our self and submit to Christ. We want to elevate ourselves, but Jesus calls us to deny ourselves. We prefer our padded, comfortable chairs at church over taking up our cross and serving as light to the world.[6]

3 James 1:22.
4 Isaiah 28:15.
5 Exodus 15:26.
6 Matthew 5:14.

Jesus calls His followers to give up their striving so they may enter God's rest. We scramble our way up life's ladder to gain what the world treasures. But when we get to the top and look around, we see a vast expanse of emptiness. The right way is found through the narrow gate that leads to a narrow path. Giving up ourselves, taking up our cross, and submitting to Christ leads us to healing and restoration for wounded souls. On our own there is no remedy for sin's sickness at any price.

> *Then Jesus said to his disciples, "Whoever wants to be my disciple must deny themselves and take up their cross and follow me. For whoever wants to save their life will lose it, but whoever loses their life for me will find it. What good will it be for someone to gain the whole world, yet forfeit their soul? Or what can anyone give in exchange for their soul?"*
> (Matthew 16:24–26)

Too many people have had their faith shipwrecked by empty promises. They need more than first-aid cream for this kind of wound. The work of the Great Commission requires spiritual warfare, and wounded souls don't have enough strength for battle. We gain the victory by rallying under our Redeemer's banner who is captain of this great salvation. Those who wander away and fall into the hands of Satan are not left hopeless. But they need major surgery to destroy cancerous flesh so that their "spirit may be saved on the day of the Lord."[7]

We are called to remain true to our calling. We must keep armored up, willing, and ready on the day of battle for the cause of Christ.[8] The kingdom work assigned to us in Jesus Christ calls us to be faithful. If we are not faithful, God is always faithful to bring us back to our calling, even if He needs to stir up a storm and send a whale to get us back on task.[9]

> *Timothy, my son, I am giving you this command in keeping with the prophecies once made about you, so that by recalling them you may fight the battle well, holding on to faith and a good conscience, which some have rejected and so have suffered shipwreck with regard to the faith.*
> (1 Timothy 1:18–19)

A gospel that marks you as a cultural Christian is only a bandage. Grace that makes you a Christian only because your family is Christian is not redemptive. Just saying you're a believer so you can get married in the church will certainly not save you. Simply sitting under the roof of a church for one hour of a worship service is not a means of salvation.

No matter what anyone tells you, even if he is a great evangelist, a charismatic preacher, or an angel, don't believe what they say unless it proves true in God's holy Scriptures. Many preachers come to proclaim their way of salvation to draw

---

7 1 Corinthians 5:5.
8 Psalm 110:3.
9 Jonah 1:17.

a crowd,[10] but the measure of gospel truth is the holy Scriptures. A spiritual salve is not the true gospel and will not heal the wounds of sin.

> *But even if we or an angel from heaven should preach a gospel other than the one we preached to you, let them be under God's curse!*
> (Galatians 1:8)

Those who press on in unbelief trip on the Cornerstone. They will die in their sins.[11] People who harbor a hidden rebellion in their hearts are hardened when they hear the gospel preached. They're like Pharoah whose heart was hardened when Moses spoke God's Word to him: "Let my people go."[12]

When hearts are steeled against Christ, their eyes are blinded to the truth. They'll stumble on the Rock, who is the stone rejected, that is, Christ Jesus. There is no other remedy for their rebellious sin.[13]

> *For in Scripture it says: "See, I lay a stone in Zion, a chosen and precious corner-stone, and the one who trusts in him will never be put to shame." Now to you who believe, this stone is precious. But to those who do not believe, "The stone the builders rejected has become the cornerstone," and, "A stone that causes people to stumble and a rock that makes them fall." They stumble because they disobey the message–which is also what they were destined for.*
> (1 Peter 2:6–8)

When you have a deep cut on your arm, the doctor will stitch it and dress the wound. Your injury needs continued care with clean dressings and ointments. Then the stitches get removed, and the wound continues to heal. If you only covered it with a bandage, your injury would not heal properly. This principle applies to the wounds of sin as well. Those who come to Jesus with repentant hearts are readily forgiven and healed of sin's wounds. The Good Shepherd restores wounded souls. He cleanses us and continues healing with generous applications of God's Word.

Listen to what John writes to his dear friend Gaius. He prayed for his good health and that he would find success and prosper, in the same way that his spiritual life flourished. It gave John great joy to hear of Gaius' faithfulness to the truth and that he continued to walk in the truth. He encouraged and strengthened his friend's faith so that he could be diligent and faithful as they "worked together for the truth."

---

10 Matthew 24:11.
11 John 8:13—24.
12 Exodus 9:12.
13 Joshua 24:19.

Dear friend, I pray that you may enjoy good health and that all may go well with you, even as your soul is getting along well. It gave me great joy when some believers came and testified about your faithfulness to the truth, telling how you continue to walk in it.

(3 John 1:2–3)

A cup of steaming hot chocolate sitting on the table in front of you has little purpose unless you inhale the sweet aroma and then sip to enjoy its woodsy, citrus flavors with subtle notes of herbs and berries. Now consider human nature that invents rituals to make you feel like you're a good person. You teach your children to pray before meals and at bedtime. Your car has an "I ♥ Jesus" bumper sticker. You wear a gold cross necklace. Your family loves church where you hear the preacher read the Bible and give a nice sermon.

These are good things to do, but if only external acts, they're like useless patches for sin's sickness, and you're among the most miserable of people.[14] If the religious things you do are like chocolate on the table that's never enjoyed, there is no healing for sin's wounds.

Instead, God's sons and daughters are called to live as children of resurrection and abide in Christ, who desires to be a living and active presence that affects your words, your footsteps, your worldview, and every aspect of everyday life. Can you hear your heavenly Father's heart breaking for you? He knows your pain and sorrows, and the desire of His heart is to rise with healing in His wings. Come, "taste and see that the Lord is good."[15]

> He heals the brokenhearted and binds up their wounds. (Psalm 147:3)

14 1 Corinthians 15:19.
15 Psalm 34:8.

Chapter 8 Q&A

A Bandage for Their Wounds

1. When you hear God's word proclaimed, what does it compel you to do?

_____

_____

_____

2. Why does our heavenly Father's heart grieve, saying, "Why then is there no healing for the wound of my people?"

_____

_____

_____

3. What is the true remedy for sin's sickness?

_____

_____

_____

4. What price did Jesus pay to heal the wounds of our transgressions?

_____

_____

_____

My Journey's Journal:

Chapter 9 : Growing Cold

Key Scriptures:

- "At that time many will turn away from the faith and will betray and hate each other, and many false prophets will appear and deceive many people. Because of the increase of wickedness, the love of most will grow cold, but the one who stands firm to the end will be saved. And this gospel of the kingdom will be preached in the whole world as a testimony to all nations, and then the end will come" (Matthew 24:11–14).

- "I know your deeds, that you are neither cold nor hot. I wish you were either one or the other! So, because you are lukewarm—neither hot nor cold—I am about to spit you out of my mouth" (Revelation 3:15–16).

Taking a hot shower after working outside all day in winter weather takes the chill out of your bones. A cold shower stimulates your body's blood flow and wakes up your senses. But lukewarm water isn't much good for anything. Barely warm coffee in your cup tastes bitter, and you want to spit it out. In the same way, spiritual apathy is repulsive.

Every headline on your news feed tells of more violence, corruption, and rampant turmoil at every turn in the road. Before long we get immune to the effects of violence and our outrage turns into complacency and finally reluctant acceptance. We become passive observers of the chaos around us. After a while, we hide away and protect ourselves with a callous indifference. Outrage dies out and apathy takes root.

But there is a better way. The Scriptures compel us to endure,[1] stand firm to the end,[2] overcome as victors in Christ,[3] continually abide in Him,[4] stand in His counsel,[5] and dwell in His dwelling place.[6] Then in the end, we will be glorified.[7]

---

1 2 Timothy 2:12.
2 Matthew 24:13.
3 1 John 5:4—6.
4 John 15:5.
5 Proverbs 19:21.
6 Psalm 23:6.
7 Colossians 3:4, 1 Peter 5:4.

> A prayer according to Galatians 6:9:
>
> Oh, Lord Almighty, strengthen us by the power of your word and your Holy Spirit so we may not be weary in well doing and endure to the end.

Esau showed an appalling indifference to his birthright as eldest son. Because of his disdain for this great treasure, he considered his growling stomach more important than the double inheritance due to him as eldest son. He sold it all for a bowl of stew to satisfy his immediate need. Those who grow cold in their faith end up like Esau, whose god was his stomach.[8]

Apathetic Christians in our day are like the first invited guests in Jesus' parable of the great banquet. They were Yahweh's holy nation but they rejected His invitation to the great wedding banquet. They had more important obligations. Their interests were short sighted and divided. They had to take care of temporal things and turned a blind eye toward eternal matters.

> *But they all alike began to make excuses. The first said, "I have just bought a field, and I must go and see it. Please excuse me." Another said, "I have just bought five yoke of oxen, and I'm on my way to try them out. Please excuse me." Still another said, "I just got married, so I can't come."*
> (Luke 14:18–20)

Complacent Christians end up feeling that God is not enough. The grass on the other side of the fence starts to look greener. We have good excuses for church hopping to find something that suits us better. The music was too contemporary, the sermons too long, and they were just a bunch of old people. Besides, the pastor had no right to correct and admonish our good friend.[9]

One major problem with the American church is that few of us submit to godly leadership, correction, or spiritual guidance. We would rather attend a church where everybody goes along to get along. Because our hearts grow cold, we prefer a church that meets our needs rather than one that leads us in true worship, teaches the whole truth of God's Word, and reveals Christ in the true gospel.

> *As I urged you when I went into Macedonia, stay there in Ephesus so that you may command certain people not to teach false doctrines any longer.*
> (1 Timothy 1:3)

True teaching suffers because we're distracted by the latest church trends. It's more interesting to debate the exact meaning of words in the Bible as we try to bend them in our favor. It's as if we're looking for loopholes in the gospel's commands. Or we may want to know if our ancestors have roots in the ancient tribes of Israel so we can feel more spiritual. We search for obscure facts about the Nephilim and create titillating teachings to excite sluggish souls.

8 Philippians 3:19.
9 2 Timothy 3:16.

We must get rid of these distractions so we can focus our energies on accomplishing the work of the great commission—the work of the church. Speculative Bible teaching is a distraction that always leave us out in the cold.

Or to devote themselves to myths and endless genealogies. Such things promote controversial speculations rather than advancing God's work–which is by faith.
(1 Timothy 1:4)

If our church manifests every spiritual gift and performs great miracles in Jesus' name, but we do not love our spouses, neighbors, and even our enemies, we're just making a lot of noise.[10] The principal command of the gospel is love that wells up from a forgiven and cleansed heart, a clear conscience, and a genuine faith. Without this fervent, Christ-like love, we're just making a lot of racket to draw attention to ourselves.

The goal of this command is love, which comes from a pure heart and a good conscience and a sincere faith.
(1 Timothy 1:5)

Sermons that promise of a life of wealth, health, and no troubles are great for satisfying itching ears. A Sunday morning message that promises a luxury car in every garage is just the one for us. Our favorite teaching is one that announces happy days for all. A prophet who speaks of better times ahead is just the one for us.[11] It's an easy trap to make "a lie our refuge and falsehood our hiding place."[12] But all temporal, earthbound pursuits leave us with empty, cold, and meaningless lives.[13]

Some have departed from these and have turned to meaningless talk.
(1 Timothy 1:6)

In this life Christians are called to carry our cross and die to self. We're compelled to give up our own plans and pursuits so that God's desires become the longing of our heart. Even in hard times, we overflow with thankfulness. We delight to see the work of God's kingdom go forward. We're constant in prayer, not only for our friends and family, but also for our church leaders and for the advancement of the gospel's message.

God's people pray in agreement with the Scriptures and each other so that we may see His will accomplished in all the earth. We're faithful to listen and test the lessons taught, the messages preached, and all prophetic words spoken to be sure they're true. We do not stifle the truth proclaimed or treat their messengers with disdain.

As faithful Bible learners we grasp the truth and hold it close, applying every word to our daily lives. People of faith recuse themselves from every kind of evil

10 1 Corinthians 13:1.
11 Micah 2:11.
12 Isaiah 28:15.
13 Ecclesiastes 1:2.

while revealing Christ to those who are bound by the chains of sin. If we don't "come out from them and be separate,[14] we become complicit with the ways of the world, and our faith grows cold.

> *Rejoice always, pray continually, give thanks in all circumstances; for this is God's will for you in Christ Jesus. Do not quench the Spirit. Do not treat prophecies with contempt but test them all; hold on to what is good, reject every kind of evil.*
> (1 Thessalonians 5:16–21)

℞

When the fire goes out, hot water turns lukewarm and then cold. Now apply this principle to our walk of faith in Jesus Christ. When we try to kindle our own fire[15] or let the fire of the Spirit go out, we end up going from hot to lukewarm and finally cold as we go through the motions of meaningless external rituals that can only help us feel good about ourselves. Then, when we get an opportunity to serve, we consider it with indifference because the Holy Spirit's fire is quenched.

When the fire of God's Holy Spirit burns bright, God's people take up their crosses, put on God's armor, and seek the Lord with all their heart, soul, and spirit. We must toss our empty, temporal, and external rituals aside and call on the Lord so we may live, serve, and minister in the fullness of Christ. Let's keep the flame in our temple burning hot and bright[16] so we may enter the joy of the Lord and bask in His holy presence.

Always be joyful. Never stop praying. Whatever happens, give thanks, because it is God's will in Christ Jesus that you do this. Don't put out the Spirit's fire. Don't despise what God has revealed. Instead, test everything. Hold on to what is good. (1 Thessalonians 5:16–21)

14 2 Corinthians 6:17.
15 Numbers 26:61.
16 Leviticus 6:13.

Chapter 9 Q&A

Growing Cold

1. What is the source of spiritual decay that causes Christians to go from hot to lukewarm and finally cold?

_____

_____

_____

2. How does a church keep from becoming little more than noisemakers?

_____

_____

_____

3. What are the dangers of being too comfortable and having everything we desire in life?

_____

_____

_____

4. We're commanded to "come out from them and be separate." What does this mean and why is it important?

_____

_____

_____

My Journey's Journal:

Chapter 10: Answer the Call

Key Scriptures:

- "Seek the Lord while he may be found; call on him while he is near" (Isaiah 55:12).

- "For he says, 'In the time of my favor I heard you, and in the day of salvation I helped you.' I tell you, now is the time of God's favor, now is the day of salvation" (2 Corinthians 6:2).

Earning our salvation is not possible, but seeking the God of our salvation is encouraged. The God of grace and mercy pursues us for a lifetime, but there is a day of salvation and a time of our Lord's favor. When this time passes, there will be no further opportunity to come to Christ. While we have ears to hear and beating hearts to receive the gospel's word of grace, this is our time to answer Jesus' knock on our heart's door. We must come to Christ, hear and believe while it is called "today," for no one knows what tomorrow holds.

Our heavenly Father's love is very enduring. He waits patiently, standing at the gate looking for us to return from our wandering ways. He longs for us to come home to His mercies. God waits even while we doze off in apathy. Our beloved knocks to awaken us so we may welcome Him. He knocks gently by means of the Word and His Holy Spirit to wake up our conscience. If our ears are stopped up, our loving Father may send troubles to jar us awake.

We must get rid of our lethargic ways and answer His call. We must answer salvation's call and the call to serve before the moment of opportunity has passed.

A prayer according to Jeremiah 29:11–14:

Heavenly Father, full of grace and truth, give us hearts that seek you so that the plans you have for us may be fulfilled. Give us a desire to call upon you and search to know you so that you may gather us into your loving arms.

Solomon's love song reveals Christ's affection for His church and the bride's love for her beloved. This love calls us to sweet communion with our Lord and Savior. Solomon's loving missal opens our ears to hear the voice of our beloved who calls out to us. But will we be too inconvenienced because we're tucked in bed, our robe is hung up for the night, and the floor is too cold for our clean, bare feet?

This was her moment, but warm and comfortable slumber held her back. Her beloved tried to open the door latch while she lingered. When she finally put her feet on the floor and went to the door, he was gone. Her heart sank, and she ran into the streets to look for him. She asked the daughters of Jerusalem to find him because her heart was "faint with love."[1] Her hesitation teaches us to stay awake and remain clothed in robes of righteousness[2] so we are ready to answer Christ's call even through the night hours.

I slept but my heart was awake. Listen! My beloved is knocking: "Open to me, my sister, my darling, my dove, my flawless one. My head is drenched with dew, my hair with the dampness of the night."
"I have taken off my robe–must I put it on again? I have washed my feet–must I soil them again?"
(Song of Songs 5:2–3)

All of God's called and chosen must stay alert to answer our Beloved's knock. We must also be discipled so we are prepared when a friend knocks on our door. We're called to, "be my witnesses in Jerusalem, and in all Judea and Samaria, and to the ends of the earth."[3] Today's mission field is first to our neighbor, to coworkers, and then to the far reaches of the earth—wherever God calls us to go. We need to be quick to the call when the guy next door comes to talk shop in the garage. His family is hungry and in need of the Bread of Life. But are we too wrapped up in our project to stop and offer him anything? If a neighbor persists in knocking at our door, will we groan, sit up, wipe the sleep from our eyes, look at the clock and groan again, and then grumble when we finally go to the door? But when we open it, our neighbor is gone. He's asking for help at someone else's door.

And suppose the one inside answers, "Don't bother me. The door is already locked, and my children and I are in bed. I can't get up and give you anything."
(Luke 11:7)

Imagine being invited to a royal wedding at Westminster Abby. After the ceremony, there's a feast with bountiful tables filled with a cornucopia of the finest food and wine. The heir to the throne will marry, and the king's generosity overflows as the wedding is prepared for the guests. How could anyone say no?

But to many, a wedding banquet seems remote and unreal. That's not our comfort zone. Besides, we have deadlines to meet. The payroll numbers must be sent out today. There's a big shipment coming in, and we have a ton of back orders to fill. We just got married, and we have reservations for our honeymoon. The excuses abound. We have real problems to deal with, so why should we let everything come to a stop? The king's son can get wedded without us. Indeed, we put what is temporal above what is eternal. But today is the day to RSVP the King's invitation.

1 Song of Songs 5:8.
2 Revelation 16:15.
3 Acts 1:8.

But they paid no attention and went off—one to his field, another to his business.
(Matthew 22:5)

The chaos of everything around us gets worse every day. Good ethics and morals are out of fashion. What was good is now bad. In fact, people applaud what is bad.[4] What used to be a kind word is considered an insult. So many people lie and greedily grab for themselves. It's a challenge to discern truth from falsehood when liars surround us. People have not only turned against a holy God, but they demand that we affirm them in their rebellion. They require us to say their lifestyles are "okay."

As the world gets crazier, we get used to it, brush it off, and begin to think of it as the new normal. We start to accept the chaos and then finally affirm it. When we compromise our values, our faith goes from hot to lukewarm and then cold. When we're caught up in the world's turmoil, it's easy to forget that today is the day for us to prepare ourselves and obey God's call to come to the wedding banquet.

We also have the prophetic message as something completely reliable, and you will do well to pay attention to it, as to a light shining in a dark place, until the day dawns and the morning star rises in your hearts.
(2 Peter 1:19)

Now that we've seen the light, we can repent of our complicity with the world. Our heavenly Father forgives and cleanses us of all unrighteousness. We're covered in Jesus' robe of righteousness, and now we can come before the throne of grace with great confidence. Our ears can hear, our eyes see the light, and we stand in God's counsel. The desire of God's heart is the very desire of our heart as we bask in the light before the throne. We rest in our Redeemer, who is our ever-present help in times of trouble.

We are cleansed and strengthened for service in God's kingdom. We're awake and on our feet, prepared for battle. God moved mountains to make the way straight for all those who put on gospel shoes. He sends them out under the authority of Christ, bolstered with great confidence.

Let us then approach God's throne of grace with confidence, so that we may receive mercy and find grace to help us in our time of need.
(Hebrews 4:16)

There is a lot of work left to do before the day Jesus returns. The church's work is not finished. Every Christian must join the harvest and do their job to complete this good work. This is your moment in time. Today is the day to answer the call to raise a banner for the nations. Don't let the sleep in your eyes blind you to the work ahead. The work of building the church isn't finished, and the time is short.

---

4 Isaiah 5:20.

Will you answer the call to put on God's armor along with those gospel shoes? Prepare yourself as a disciple of Christ and then go out to lift up Christ and the cross to a world torn by sin's chaos.

You too, be patient and stand firm, because the Lord's coming is near.
(James 5:8)

The work of the church is the Great Commission, and it's a tireless endeavor. The apostle Paul admonished the Galatian church: "Let us not become weary in doing good, for at the proper time we will reap a harvest if we do not give up."[5] The saints are called to press on in their calling, each one doing their part, and working together.

Paul encourages us to seek the Lord, follow his example, pursue our eternal purpose in Christ, and win the prize. It's essential that we seek the Lord and encourage each other every day to keep us from complacency. We must not harden our hearts toward this good work.[6] Tomorrow doesn't belong to us. Today is our day to shine out with the light of Christ.

As you know, we count as blessed those who have persevered. You have heard of Job's perseverance and have seen what the Lord finally brought about. The Lord is full of compassion and mercy.
(James 5:11)

A blazing light dawns to pierce through the dark clouds of chaos. The darkness of sin defiles earth, pressing in from every side. Arise, oh Lord, and drive back the pressing darkness so that we may see Christ in our time. Give us hearts that answer salvation's call and then respond to your appeal to do the work of your kingdom.

Will we grasp the moment and answer the Lord's call in the day of His favor? Will we brush away our slumber, open our eyes, and rise to answer His call? When the morning star rises in our hearts, it is our time to put our feet on the floor and answer the call. If we slumber, our season of favor will pass.

> I press on toward the goal to win the prize for which God has called me heavenward in Christ Jesus. (Philippians 3:14)

---

5 Galatians 6:9.
6 Hebrews 3:13.

Chapter 10 Q&A

Answer the Call

1. Why is it so hard for us to answer our Beloved's call when we're all tucked in, warm and comfortable?

_____

_____

_____

2. Is it really that important for us to constantly be dressed and ready?

_____

_____

_____

3. What excuses keep people from accepting the wedding invitation?

_____

_____

_____

4. What are the consequences of hesitating in your comfort zone and missing today's call?

_____

_____

_____

My Journey's Journal:

Part III
The Road of Suffering

"I consider that our present sufferings are not worth comparing with the glory that will be revealed in us."
(Romans 8:18)

When Christ sets our feet free to run on His narrow pathway, we must count the cost. What do we have to give up to follow in Jesus' footsteps in the way of suffering?

Chapter 11: By Grace Through Faith Alone

Key Scriptures:

- "For all have sinned and fall short of the glory of God, and all are justified freely by his grace through the redemption that came by Christ Jesus" (Romans 3:23-24).

- "Therefore, the promise comes by faith, so that it may be by grace and may be guaranteed to all Abraham's offspring—not only to those who are of the law but also to those who have the faith of Abraham. He is the father of us all" (Romans 4:16).

Every Christian should have the experience of herding sheep in open pastures. The ewes and lambs will confirm God's Word that we're all wanderers. Lambs tend to forget the safety of the fold and cross boundaries as they go in search of greener pastures. The rams are aggressive and test the shepherd's guidance. They all need a shepherd who knows them by name, goes out to search for those who are lost, and calls them to the safety of His sheepfold.

The Good Shepherd searches and finds us where we are caught in our sins. He knows we have no strength left in us to call out to Him. Then He calls out to us, and by the power of the Word, the Spirit of Christ plants the seed of faith in the hearts of all those who are called and chosen. By the power of the Word and the Holy Spirit, He gives us ears to hear life-giving words. He gathers us into a fellowship of faith where we hear the Word that waters the seed of faith to make us grow in the grace and knowledge of our Lord and Savior, Jesus Christ.

> A prayer according to John 1:16–18:
>
> Oh, God of our salvation, lead us to the fullness of your grace upon grace, the grace and truth that is ours through Jesus Christ who reveals to us our heavenly Father's loving and forgiving nature.

Cold rain drops seeped through the tent onto a shivering homeless man in his soaked sleeping bag. Chuck ran his grubby fingers through his greasy blond hair to get ready for another day. Then he drank his last sip of water and ate the last bite of granola bar he had saved in its wrapper. His stomach growled. His cell phone battery was dead. He checked again, but he couldn't find even one penny in his pocket. Then, through the *drip, drip, drip,* he heard an echo of a still and quiet voice calling to him.

Come, all you who are thirsty, come to the waters; and you who have no money, come, buy and eat! Come, buy wine and milk without money and without cost.
(Isaiah 55:1)

You don't have to be homeless to get lost along life's way. It's easier for a man of wealth and renown to take the wrong road. Consider Charles, alone in his master suite with his mind spinning as he tries to rest under his embroidered sateen sheets. He's tried everything, but misery sticks to him like a wet blanket. His heart feels like a cold, hard rock in his chest.

Then it's like someone turned on a light. He remembers an old Bible his mother willed to him. He gets out of bed and rustles around in his walk-in closet until he finds it. He opens the well-worn pages, and there before his eyes is a verse that his mother had highlighted.

Jesus answered, "I am the way and the truth and the life. No one comes to the Father except through me."
(John 14:6)

Right before his eyes, Charles sees Christ revealed to him in the words of his mom's old Bible. A sense of his mother's faith reaches out to him through the holy Scriptures he holds in his hands. The roots of his father's faith come alive inside him. By the power of the word, the Holy Spirit plants the seed of faith in his heart.

Charles flips through the pages with a ravenous hunger.

Therefore, the promise comes by faith, so that it may be by grace and may be guaranteed to all Abraham's offspring—not only to those who are of the law but also to those who have the faith of Abraham. He is the father of us all.
(Romans 4:16)

Charles' cell phone interrupts him with a chime, making him realize he has an appointment at the office. He sends a quick text, takes a three-minute shower, shaves, brushes his perfectly trimmed blond hair, puts on his dress shirt and favorite paisley tie, a pinstriped suit, wing-tip shoes, and he is in the car on his way.

But then, while taking a corner too fast, the low-air pressure light comes on. He pulls onto the shoulder, looks at his tires, throws up his hands and exclaims, "I've never changed a tire before, and I'm already late."

But this was the right moment, at the right time, and the right place. A raggedy man sitting on a tree stump at the roadside clears his throat with a sputtering growl and calls out, "Aye-hem. Need help?"

You see, at just the right time, when we were still powerless, Christ died for the ungodly. Very rarely will anyone die for a righteous person, though for a good person someone might possibly dare to die. But God demonstrates his own love for us in this:

While we were still sinners, Christ died for us.
(Romans 5:6–8)

While Chuck changes the flat tire, Charles grabs his mom's Bible from the front seat and starts reading aloud. "Not because of anything we have done." He looks at Chuck, who holds a handful of lug nuts. "I thought I was okay with God because I've got everything I need and a lot of things I want."

Chuck turns to size up Charles in his pinstriped suit. "At least I know I got troubles with the man upstairs."

"Look, read this." Charles holds out the Bible to Chuck.

"I can't. My glasses got stolen."

"Well, you're all finished, so let's go get a pair of glasses for you. You have to read this." Charles offers a white handkerchief for Chuck to wipe his grimy hands. "You gotta read this."

He has saved us and called us to a holy life–not because of anything we have done but because of his own purpose and grace. This grace was given us in Christ Jesus before the beginning of time, but it has now been revealed through the appearing of our Savior, Christ Jesus, who has destroyed death and has brought life and immortality to light through the gospel.
(2 Timothy 1:9–10)

Chuck and Charles sit at a corner table in the diner. The Bible is open in front of them, and their excitement builds as they read all of Mom's underlined Scriptures.

"I used to have a Bible, but it got lost along the way. Along with my job, my house, and my family." Chuck's thoughts drift to another time, as he sips his coffee and looks out the window as if to watch it all blow away.

"I've had a Bible all this time, but I had stored it away. I never cared to read it." Charles signals the waitress to refill their coffee mugs.

"It feels like Jesus is tuggin' on my heart. You too?"

"Yes, it started just before I found my mom's old Bible this morning. It's like I heard Jesus calling me." Charles looks over his breakfast companion's scruffy coat with pine needles still clinging to it. "Hey, there's a nice space in my carriage house. Why don't you stay there? We'll go to church Sunday morning." Charles brushed away Chuck's wide-eyed shock. "Oh, no problem. I'm glad I met you today. You know what? It was the right time to have a flat tire."

Behold, I stand at the door and knock. If anyone hears my voice and opens the door, I will come in to him and eat with him, and he with me.
(Revelation 3:20 ESV)

A revelation of Jesus Christ draws both rich and poor to Christ as they read and hear God's Word. The Scriptures opened their eyes to see their Redeemer and their need of a Savior. Then, by the grace of our Lord Jesus, the seed of faith was planted in their hearts. They tasted the Bread of Life and saw that the Lord is good. The Spirit of life gave them a ravenous hunger for more of God's Word. A desire for fellowship with other Christians soon followed.

Impoverished people are not the only ones who to get lost along the way. Wealth, good health, and comfort tend to blind people to the impoverished condition of their soul. Affluence tends to keep people from seeing their need of Christ. It's hard for derelict men and impoverished women to see a way to get free from the chains of sin's darkness. But no matter their status, people who hear God's Word, receive, and believe the Good News come face to face with the Way, the Truth, and the Life. God's forgiveness and mercy remove the weight of riches and chains of poverty forever.

> Many are the plans in a person's heart, but it is the Lord's purpose that prevails.
> (Proverbs 19:21)

Chapter 11 Q&A

By Grace Through Faith Alone

1. How does the Spirit of Christ draw us out of our lost condition?

_____

_____

_____

2. How is it possible for people to end up in the right place at the right time?

_____

_____

_____

3. Why do people hunger for more when they get a taste of the Bread of Life?

_____

_____

_____

My Journey's Journal:

Chapter 12: All Have Sinned

Key Scriptures:

- "The Lord looks down from heaven on all mankind to see if there are any who understand, any who seek God. All have turned away, all have become corrupt; there is no one who does good, not even one" (Psalm 14:2–3).

- "Who can say, 'I have kept my heart pure; I am clean and without sin?'" (Proverbs 20:9).

When we walk barefoot on a sandy beach and pick up a little seashell, we feel like the world is our oyster. The tiny shell that washed up from the sea gives us a sense of being big enough to go anywhere and do anything. But then we turn and see the vast expanse of ocean that stretches beyond the horizon, and we feel so small. In the same way, when we compare ourselves with others, we might feel good about who we are. But when we come face to face with the Word and "grasp how wide and long and high and deep is the love of Christ,"[1] we see our weaknesses and our need of Christ. Our spiritual poverty becomes evident in the light of God's only Son.

It's so easy to justify ourselves and think we're good enough to get to heaven. Comparing our way of life with certain people helps us feel that we're not so bad after all—we don't do recreational drugs, never had a DUI, and we don't curse at our neighbors. We go to church and we're a good person. We teach Sunday school and feel respectable. The good things we do for our family and church can make it easy to forget that we're fallible sinners in need of constant grace, forgiveness, and mercy. We need to be reminded that our natural bent is toward corruption.

A prayer according to Ephesians 1:18:

Spirit of Grace, open our eyes to see our sin. Bring our hearts to repentance and then enlighten us so we may know the hope you have given us as a glorious inheritance.

Eyes with 20/20 vision can be blind to the truth. If we exalt ourselves in our own eyes, it's easy to justify our wrong attitude toward others. Overlooking our own sin is easy when we're busy pointing out others' wrongdoing.[2] If we spend our time working on a fix for other people's problems, we don't have to work on

1 Ephesians 3:18.
2 Matthew 7:3—5.

our own issues. Talking about everything that's wrong with our church and our pastor relives us of the burden of thinking about how we contributed to the problems. Complaining about our rowdy neighbors keeps us from having to confront our own hostile attitudes. But these arrogant attitudes lead to destruction.

In their own eyes they flatter themselves too much to detect or hate their sin.
(Psalm 36:2)

We're born into a corrupt world. We enter the world by the will of the flesh, but we're dead in our sins and need to be reborn of God.[3] Only one perfect person walked on planet earth—the perfect Lamb of God who came in the flesh as Immanuel to shed His life blood to take away the sins of the world. He came in the flesh and gave His body to be broken to heal us of sin's corruption—restored in body, soul, and spirit. We need Christ who gives us His righteousness as our own.

Everyone has turned away, all have become corrupt; there is no one who does good, not even one.
(Psalm 53:3)

The prophet Isaiah offers us a great perspective on the sin of fallen mankind. He likens us to sheep who have wandered away to find greener pastures. Depraved minds dream up new ways to spread sin's chaos. We live in a world that's every man for himself in a jungle that is rife with pitfalls and traps. Injustice becomes the new normal as we focus on our own advancement and interests. There is no truth in us. We lie when the truth would serve better. We abandon true worship, turning to external religious rites and entrenched traditions. But our Lord Jesus Christ came as Immanuel and took upon himself the sins of every one of us. He came in the flesh and paid our sin debt in full. He died in our place and for our sins to set us free.

We all, like sheep, have gone astray, each of us has turned to our own way; and the Lord has laid on him the iniquity of us all.
(Isaiah 53:6)

People like to look their best when they come to church. Our clean faces smile big when we walk through the door. Our hair is neat and tidy. We carry a big Bible with a lot of markers and underlined verses. But if we opened our Bible and allowed its light to shine into the deepest recesses of our hearts, it would expose the corruption in our lives. The light of Christ reveals our showy righteous acts as nothing but filth. We put on our best face for church, but then the light of the Word reveals that we are spiritually torn, lame, sick, and in need of Christ. Our best efforts to serve the church by our own means are proven to be little more that wood, hay, and stubble that cannot pass the test of fire.[4] We want to appear as green leaves on a fruitful tree, but we're fallen leaves that shrivel in the heat of day and get swept away in the winds of night. We're in serious need of Christ.

3 John 1:13.
4 1 Corinthians 3:12—13.

80

All of us have become like one who is unclean, and all our righteous acts are like filthy rags; we all shrivel up like a leaf, and like the wind our sins sweep us away.
(Isaiah 64:6)

We're given a touchstone that we must use to measure our lives. God's Word is the benchmark for all things. God's perfection is the standard.[5] God's justice is our measuring line, and His righteousness is the plumb line we use to check our lives.[6]

With the means of measuring in hand, it becomes obvious that none of us measures up. In our despair, we turn from our own good efforts and put our faith in Christ Jesus, our righteousness. He wraps us in His robe of righteousness and ushers us into God's holy presence, saying, "This is your adopted son, this is your adopted daughter who are now called by your holy name. I've forgiven them and wrapped them in my righteousness."

We are made right with God by placing our faith in Jesus Christ. And this is true for everyone who believes, no matter who we are. For everyone has sinned; we all fall short of God's glorious standard.
(Romans 3:23 NLT)

We all need to think of ourselves as good people. It's always possible to find someone who is worse than us so we can compare and feel okay about who we are. We don't lie like Larry. We don't cheat at cards like Chip. We don't leave our kids at home alone like Lilly does. We simply deceive ourselves with a false standard. There is no truth in us. We believe the fiction we create for ourselves.

The reality is that when we use any other measure for our lives to make us look good, we call God a liar and there is no truth in us. God's Word calls us to repent of our self-justifying deceptions. When we confess our sin and our sinfulness, God is faithful. He not only forgives us of our sin, but He also cleanses us of all unrighteousness, because He is just and righteous.

If we claim to be without sin, we deceive ourselves and the truth is not in us. If we confess our sins, he is faithful and just and will forgive us our sins and purify us from all unrighteousness. If we claim we have not sinned, we make him out to be a liar and his word is not in us.
(1 John 1:8–10)

Will you compare yourself to your neighbor so you can say, "I'm good enough. I'm okay?" Your coworkers, friends, and baseball buddies can't pro-

5 Matthew 5:48.
6 Isaiah 28:17.

vide a proper standard of righteousness. Because of Adam's fall in the garden, we're all born with sin's stain and delivered into a sin-bent world. The dominion of darkness drags us down into the dregs of sin. We must not deny our sin but confess our sin, sinfulness, and our need of Christ. Our hearts ought to break because of our offenses. In repentance we have a great hope. Christ, who delivers us and breaks the power of sin is our hope—an eternal hope.

> We know that our old sinful selves were crucified with Christ so that sin might lose its power in our lives. We are no longer slaves to sin. (Romans 6:6)

Chapter 12 Q&A

All Have Sinned

1. Why is it important to examine ourselves to keep corruption from unwittingly weaseling its way in over time?

_____

_____

_____

2. What distractions do we use to divert our attention from our own sin and failings?

_____

_____

_____

3. What is the natural bend of all mankind?

_____

_____

_____

4. Where do we find the standard of measure we must use to check up on ourselves?

_____

_____

_____

My Journey's Journal:

Chapter 13: The Way of the Cross

Key Scriptures:

- "Jesus answered, 'I am the way and the truth and the life. No one comes to the Father except through me'" (John 14:6).

- "This is good, and pleases God our Savior, who wants all people to be saved and to come to a knowledge of the truth. For there is one God and one mediator between God and mankind, the man Christ Jesus, who gave himself as a ransom for all people. This has now been witnessed to at the proper time" (1 Timothy 2:3–4).

When you're caught in the clutches of student loan debt, credit card debt, payments on a car, and rent increases you can't afford, it adds up to crushing troubles. You feel like you're drowning in a sea of liabilities. You need a financial miracle. The first step is to lay all it out so you can see the full scope of your overwhelming problem. Then look up to where your help comes from.[1] Our heavenly Father established a principle called Jubilee, when debts are forgiven and property is restored. Jesus came in the flesh, proclaimed His Jubilee, and paid the price for sin's debt.

Our Lord and Savior, Jesus Christ paid the price of redemption in full for all people. His desire is for all of us to come to saving faith. He paid the price to redeem all lost souls from sin's death penalty.[2] Now free from sin's curse, we are called to present Christ as the way, and the truth, and the life. By means of the Word and the Holy Spirit, He reveals Himself to lost souls. He gives ears to hear and hearts to believe. We proclaim the way of the cross that makes us new creations and restores life to our body, soul, and spirit.

> A prayer according to Colossians 2:13–14:
>
> Lord Jesus our Savior, you found us when we were dead in our sins and bound by the flesh. Then you made us new creations, alive in Christ. Thank you for paying our sin debt in full and nailing it to the cross.

One of the most pleasant moments in life is to hold your newborn baby snuggled in your arms. The joy of it inspires a love song to flow from your heart to

---

1 Psalm 121:1—2.
2 Romans 6:23.

your child. Your newborn baby is perfectly beautiful. The child we hold seems so innocent and pure. But reality is that all children are born into a sin-bent world. They must grow up in states and nations that are corrupted with injustice.

But we have a God is mighty to save.[3] He is mighty in battle.[4] We serve an awesome God who sent His only Son who came in the flesh to walk among us, teach us, heal us, and then give His life to redeem us from sin's bondage. In Christ, justice overrules all injustice. Our Lord and Savior has overcome the world and gathers a remnant in whom He delights. He makes us new creations in Christ and sings a love song as He saves us from sin's clutches.

> *The Lord your God is with you, the Mighty Warrior who saves. He will take great delight in you; in his love he will no longer rebuke you, but will rejoice over you with singing.*
> (Zephaniah 3:17)

There is only one gate, one door, one way to be saved, and that is Jesus Christ. Our Lord and Savior leads us into all truth and life. But we're poor, weary, lame, and enslaved by sin's debt. We have no strength of our own to enter His narrow gate. We're dead in our sins. Our ears can't hear. Our eyes can't see. But when God's Word is proclaimed, our eyes are opened, our ears begin to hear the Holy Spirit who reveals Christ, and plants the seed of faith in our hearts.[5] The Good Shepherd leads us through the gate to save our lost souls. He guides us into the safety of His fold and then leads us to His green pastures.

> *I am the gate; whoever enters through me will be saved. They will come in and go out, and find pasture.*
> (John 10:9)

People are very inventive when it comes to justifying themselves. We tend to search for something greater than ourselves that can lift us up and save us from that empty void in our hearts. We often fill that vacuum with all kinds of distractions. But our efforts amount to empty trivialities.

With an overwhelming love, Jesus answered Thomas' doubts, saying, "I am the way and the truth and the life. No one comes to the Father except through me."[6] His holy and awesome name is Yeshua HaMashiach.[7] He is more than able to save us. He came in the flesh and gave His body to be broken to make us whole in body, soul, and spirit. He came as a man and gave His blood to be shed on a cruel Roman cross to cleanse and wash us whiter than fresh fallen snow.[8] Jesus provided the only way to saving grace, and it's an amazing, beautiful path.

---

3 Isaiah 63:1.
4 Psalm 24:8.
5 Romans 10:17.
6 John 14:6.
7 Yeshua HaMashiach means The Anointed One and Jesus the Messiah.
8 Psalm 51:7.

Salvation is found in no one else, for there is no other name under heaven given to mankind by which we must be saved.
(Acts 4:12)

No one can come on their own to stand in the presence of our heavenly Father. We must first make peace with the Almighty. That peace is only possible through Jesus Christ, the Son of God. By grace through faith, the blood of the Lamb of God that was shed on our behalf now justifies us and makes peace with the Great I AM. Jesus wraps us in His robe of righteousness and ushers us into His Father's presence. He reveals the knowledge of His glory so we may delight in our great hope—the God of our salvation.

Therefore, since we have been justified through faith, we have peace with God through our Lord Jesus Christ, through whom we have gained access by faith into this grace in which we now stand. And we boast in the hope of the glory of God.
(Romans 5:1–3)

A dramatic change takes place in a church when Jesus is Lord of every Christian's life. It's right and good to lead people to saving grace and then teach them that God desires to be King in their lives.

When we lead people to Christ, it's misleading if we make the way easier by saying, "just believe in Jesus as Savior—it's not about your lifestyle." Instead, we must lead them in the way of the cross, to believe in Jesus Christ as Savior, and then be discipled so He is Lord of every part of their lives.

Those who come to saving faith are commanded to be baptized into the name of the Father, Son, and Holy Spirit. Then as newborn children of the Most High God they become hungry for God's Word so they may grow in love and obedience. This is vital to their walk of faith because if Jesus is not Lord over a Christian's life, they're limited to doing what right in their own eyes.[9]

Without Christ as Lord, we're no better off than the Israelites ruled by judges. They were called by God's holy name. They were part of God's holy nation, but they refused God as their King and lived according to their own standards.

Our love of Christ compels us to obey Him. A true walk of faith becomes evident as God's grace reigns in us through righteousness. He strengthens us by the power of the Word and the Holy Spirit to endure to the end and enter eternal life.

So that, just as sin reigned in death, so also grace might reign through righteousness to bring eternal life through Jesus Christ our Lord.
(Romans 5:21)

Consider the work that Jesus' cross accomplishes in our lives. He paid our sin debt in full. Now we can feed on God's Word, our hearts are contrite before the Lord, we're covered by the blood, and wrapped in Jesus' robe of righteousness. We

9 Judges 17:6, 21:25.

can come with great confidence before our Heavenly Father who is holy. Our High Priest, Jesus Christ, makes a way for us to enter the awesome presence of the Great I AM. With the heart and mind of Christ, and with the assurance of our salvation, we come to worship on Mount Zion, the city of the living God. We join the angels festive gathering. Faith in Jesus Christ ushers us into gatherings of the faithful whose names are written in the Book of Life.[10] This is the way of the cross.

> *Therefore, brothers and sisters, since we have confidence to enter the Most Holy Place by the blood of Jesus, by a new and living way opened for us through the curtain, that is, his body, and since we have a great priest over the house of God, let us draw near to God with a sincere heart and with the full assurance that faith brings, having our hearts sprinkled to cleanse us from a guilty conscience and having our bodies washed with pure water.*
> (Hebrews 10:19–22)

People get a bit thirsty while they skate along life's easy street. They're looking for something to wet their thirst when a narrow gate enlightens their searching eyes. It's like a treasure hidden among the grapevines growing around it.[11] Then they hear a voice calling out their name, "Are you thirsty? Come and drink." But that narrow gate isn't very attractive.[12] The gate has no bright lights or flashing neon signs. It doesn't advertise or offer them the break they deserve. Their minds race: "There must be a better way to satisfy my thirst."

They keep looking around, not knowing what they're looking for. They are blind to the one gate, one door, and one way that forever satisfies their thirst. How can they know when they're not even asking? How can they find a Savior when they're not seeking one?[13]

A way is provided for them to see that Jesus Christ is holding out His nail scarred hands to them. They need a witness of our Savior's grace. They need a friend to proclaim Christ who alone paid the price to release the poor, weary, lame, thirsty, and those bound by sin's debt. They're dead in their sins and there's no life in them. How can they come to enter Jesus' narrow gate? Dead people can't hear or see.

But when God's Word is proclaimed, the Holy Spirit gives them eyes to see and quickens their ears so they can hear. The Spirit of Christ plants the seed of faith in their hearts.[14] The Good Shepherd holds out His hands to them, and

10 Hebrews 12:22—24.
11 Proverbs 2:4.
12 Isaiah 53:2.
13 Isaiah 65:1.
14 Romans 10:17.

His love song draws them to come and drink from the waters of life so they will never thirst again.

> He came and preached peace to you who were far away and peace to those who were near. For through him we both have access to the Father by one Spirit.
> (Ephesians 2:17–18)

Chapter 13 Q&A

The Way of the Cross

1. If a person is deaf, blind, lame, and dead in their sins, is there any hope?

_____

_____

_____

2. How do we make peace with our heavenly Father so we may come into His holy presence?

_____

_____

_____

3. How does a newborn Christian grow and mature in grace and knowledge of Christ?

_____

_____

_____

4. What is the source of our confidence as we enter the Most Holy Place?

_____

_____

_____

My Journey's Journal:

Chapter 14: The Essence of the Gospel

Key Scriptures:

- "For what I received I passed on to you as of first importance: that Christ died for our sins according to the Scriptures, that he was buried, that he was raised on the third day according to the Scriptures" (1 Corinthians 15:3–4).

- "But also for us, to whom God will credit righteousness—for us who believe in him who raised Jesus our Lord from the dead. He was delivered over to death for our sins and was raised to life for our justification" (Romans 4:24–25).

When a newborn baby takes her first breath, that's just the beginning of many years of life. They must be fed, cuddled, talked to, nurtured, trained, disciplined, and taught. A good parent doesn't look at their baby and say, "Well, I guess we'll see how this one turns out." Children don't have a life because they took one breath of air. They're brought into a lifetime of teaching and loving discipline that helps them grow up. They make mistakes, and parents use them as teaching moments.

Salvation is more like a pilgrimage than a one-time event. There is a moment of joy when Christ is revealed to us, but that's just the beginning of a joy-filled life in Christ. We're baptized and then discipled. Growing in grace and knowledge in not an easy road, and because of this it's so important for the Scriptures to offer us great assurance of our salvation.[1] God's Word encourages us to endure to the end to be saved.[2]

We are justified (proclaimed not guilty) by grace and through faith alone. Continual washing in the Word sanctifies Christians. God's children anticipate being glorified when Christ returns for His own. We rejoice to see that glorious day when we will be like Him and see Him as He is.[3] We are justified, getting sanctified, and will be glorified. Simply said; by faith we are saved, by faith Christ is saving us, and by faith we will be saved. Working in threes is the way of God's kingdom.

---

1 John 10:28.
2 Matthew 24:13.
3 1 John 3:2.

A prayer according to 1 John 3:2:

God of our fathers, you have adopted us as your children, and yet what we will be you have yet to fully reveal. Give us hearts that treasure the hope of our salvation as we wait for the day when Jesus Christ appears, and we will see that we are like Him and see Him as He is.

Justification

This righteousness is given through faith in Jesus Christ to all who believe. There is no difference between Jew and Gentile, for all have sinned and fall short of the glory of God, and all are justified freely by his grace through the redemption that came by Christ Jesus.
(Romans 3:22–24)

No one can come to the Father apart from a revelation of His Son.[4] When our eyes are opened to see our Savior, our ears hear God's Word, and our minds understand; we come into peace with God through faith in Jesus Christ.[5] This great salvation is ours by grace through faith alone.

What is this faith? It is the assurance of what we cannot see with our natural eyes.[6] What is our hope? It is confidence in what we do not yet have but look forward to with great expectation. The faith planted in us is like a seed that must be watered and fed to make it grow; first a sprout, then a stem, next a green head forms, and finally the ripened kernels of wheat are ready for harvest.

We die with Christ in the waters of baptism. We're buried with Christ in baptismal water. New creations are joined with Christ in resurrection power when lifted from the water—baptized into the name of the Father, Son, and Holy Spirit.

Paul likened the work of salvation to a seed planted in the ground. The seed dies in the soil and then sprouts and grows to bear good fruit.[7] We become adopted as sons and daughters of the Most High God, given a new family name, sealed with a promise of eternal life, and then nurtured to make us ready for the harvest.

He also said, "This is what the kingdom of God is like. A man scatters seed on the ground. Night and day, whether he sleeps or gets up, the seed sprouts and grows, though he does not know how. All by itself the soil produces grain—first the stalk, then the head, then the full kernel in the head. As soon as the grain is ripe, he puts the sickle to it, because the harvest has come."
(Mark 4:26–29).

---

4 1 Corinthians 2:9—10.
5 Romans 5:1.
6 Hebrews 11:1.
7 1 Corinthians 15:36.

The apostle Peter wrote in his epistle to warn Christians to be on their guard against the erroneous teaching of lawless men that would cause them to fall from their secure position in Christ. Yes, it is possible to fall away, wander away, or be led away from God's saving grace. We were once wild olive branches but are now grafted into the Tree of Life. The Scriptures warn us that unfruitful branches are cut off and thrown into the fire.[8] But those who keep His commands and endure in fruitfulness to the end will be kept from the hour of trial. For those who are not faithful, God is faithful. They may yet be saved, but like smoldering sticks snatched from the fire.[9]

Since you have kept my command to endure patiently, I will also keep you from the hour of trial that is going to come on the whole world to test the inhabitants of the earth. (Revelation 3:10)

Those who are born of God become hungry for more of Christ. They feast on the Word. They stand with Paul, saying, "I want to know Christ—yes, to know the power of his resurrection and participation in his sufferings, becoming like him in his death, and so, somehow, attaining to the resurrection from the dead."[10]

By grace and through faith alone we are justified and given right standing before God who is holy. We didn't earn it. God doesn't choose us because we're good enough. There is nothing we can do to deserve God's saving grace. We don't have to live a holy life before we can be justified. We cannot and must not depend on our own righteousness but on the righteousness of Jesus Christ alone. But God called us and chose us to live in keeping with repentance. He justifies us by means of Christ and the cross to prepare the way for us to move forward into sanctification.

For it is by grace you have been saved, through faith—and this is not from yourselves, it is the gift of God—not by works, so that no one can boast. (Ephesians 2:8–9).

Sanctification

For this very reason, make every effort to add to your faith goodness; and to goodness, knowledge; and to knowledge, self-control; and to self-control, perseverance; and to perseverance, godliness; and to godliness, mutual affection; and to mutual affection, love. For if you possess these qualities in increasing measure, they will keep you from being ineffective and unproductive in your knowledge of our Lord Jesus Christ. (2 Peter 1:5–8)

---

8 Romans 11:17—24.
9 Zechariah 3:2, Jude 1:23.
10 Philippians 3:10—11.

Sanctification will not be done for you, and you cannot do it on your own. Godliness requires personal effort,[11] yet it is the work of the Spirit.[12] Your own efforts cannot justify you, but searching is encouraged.[13] Sanctification is the "work out your salvation," and the abide in Christ part of being saved.[14] It's the "grow in grace and knowledge" stage of redemption.[15] You're in the "cleanse yourself" part that comes by repentance and by getting saturated in the Word.[16] This is the "make every effort" part of saving faith.[17] Sanctification conforms you to the Word. This stage of your Christian walk helps you continue in God's kindness.[18]

Those who are being sanctified listen to the apostle Paul's encouragement and press on in their faith. We pay attention to the apostle Peter who encourages us to gain Christ in increasing measure to keep from becoming complacent in our walk of faith. To be sanctified, we must fight the good fight of faith to take hold of eternal life,[19] to make our calling and election sure.[20] A desire to learn and do what God requires burns in the hearts of all who are being conformed to Christ.

Not that I have already obtained all this, or have already arrived at my goal, but I press on to take hold of that for which Christ Jesus took hold of me. (Philippians 3:12)

We are encouraged to exercise and strengthen our faith by growing in our knowledge of Christ. It's as if the Lord gives us one small talent and responsibility to start our faith-strengthening program. Then when we're ready, He gives us greater talents and bigger tasks to exercise our faith. We grow in grace and knowledge as we apply God's Word to our lives. Maturing Christians obey the gospel and live our lives according to truth, righteousness, and in the fear of the Lord. Exercising our faith by doing good deeds will not save us. We're fruitful because we are God's people who are made part of Christ's royal priesthood. The good fruit we produce is the result of being grafted into and remaining in the Vine, who is Christ Jesus.

Remain in me, as I also remain in you. No branch can bear fruit by itself; it must remain in the vine. Neither can you bear fruit unless you remain in me. (John 15:4)

A Christian husband can't save his wife and family, but he sanctifies their marital and family relationships when he serves as a minister of righteousness in his home. In the same way, a believing wife can't justify her unbelieving husband

---

11 2 Peter 3:14.
12 Galatians 5:22—24.
13 Matthew 6:33.
14 Philippians 2:12.
15 2 Peter 3:18.
16 2 Timothy 2:21, Ephesians 5:26.
17 Hebrews 4:11, 12:14
18 Romans 11:22.
19 1 Timothy 6:11—12.
20 2 Peter 1:10—11.

but serves to sanctify their marriage as she ministers Christ to her family.

In a very real sense, Mom and Dad serve with covenantal acts that are like giving their family the "the shirt off their back." Living together in a loving family serves to shape and refine us. Our sacrificial acts of service to our spouse, children, and neighbors show that God's Word is constantly being applied to our lives to effect godliness. Loving discipline and tender nurturing of those in our care reflects the Word at work in our hearts and minds to sanctify us. We seek the Lord who makes us holy us as we look forward to our glorification.

For the unbelieving husband has been sanctified through his wife, and the unbeliev-
ing wife has been sanctified through her believing husband. Otherwise your children
would be unclean, but as it is, they are holy.
(1 Corinthians 7:14)[21]

Glorification

For now we see only a reflection as in a mirror; then we shall see face to face. Now I
know in part; then I shall know fully, even as I am fully known.
(1 Corinthians 13:12)

There's a beautiful old hymn of the church that many congregations sing with great hope. Aging voices sing this song with greater fervor and understanding after many years of life's hardships and troubles.

> "When all my labors and trials are o'er,
> And I am safe on that beautiful shore,
> Just to be near the dear Lord I adore
> Will through the ages be glory for me.
>
> O that will be glory for me,
> Glory for me, glory for me;
> When by His grace I shall look at His face,
> That will be glory, be glory for me."[22]

By means of God's saving grace, our Lord Jesus Christ gives us a sense of belonging as He unites us with a family of faith in His church. This sense of security gives us great hope, and this hope opens our eyes to see beyond the day we die and cross the threshold into eternity. We, like Adam, will come to the end of our days. Then, after we take our last breath, God's holy angels carry us into Christ's presence.[23]

---

21 Additional study Scriptures: Isaiah 7:9b, Romans 6:22, 1 Thessalonians 4:4, 1 Thessalonians 5:23, 2 Thessa-
    lonians 2:13, 1 Timothy 4:7–8, 2 Timothy 4:8, Titus 2:13–14, Hebrews 12:14, James 1:25, 2 John 1:9.
22 Author: Chas. H. Gabriel. From the *African Methodist Episcopal Church Hymnal*. (Public domain)
23 Luke 16:22, 2 Corinthians 5:8.

By the first man, Adam, death came into the world. In the second Adam, Jesus Christ, we are raised up to eternal life.[24] Because Christ is risen as the firstfruits of resurrection, all those who are in Christ will be raised up in resurrection power. We can stand shoulder to shoulder with the apostle Paul and declare: "Where, O death, is your victory? Where, O death, is your sting?"[25] With grateful hearts we shout out with praise: "But thanks be to God! He gives us the victory through Jesus Christ.[26]

For as in Adam all die, so in Christ all will be made alive. But each in turn: Christ, the firstfruits; then, when he comes, those who belong to him.
(1 Corinthians 15:22–23).

Through all the years of our life, hope strengthens us so we may glory in our sufferings. This is possible because "we know that suffering produces perseverance; perseverance character, and character hope."[27] In this eternal hope we will never be disappointed or shamed, "because God's love has been poured out into our hearts through the Holy Spirit, who has been given to us."[28] In every moment of life's troubles, we can look forward to the day Christ appears and His holy angels carry us into His glory.

Bodies sown in corruption are raised in incorruption. They are sown in dishonor but raised in glory. We are planted in weakness and then raised in power. We were born with a natural body, and then we will have a spiritual body like His. This is possible because the last Adam became a life-giving Spirit.[29] We were born in the image of the earthly man, Adam, and we will be resurrected in the image of the heavenly man, Jesus Christ.[30]

When Christ, who is your life, appears, then you also will appear with him in glory.
(Colossians 3:4)

Heaven does not print its citizenship documents with perishable ink and paper. Instead, the Holy Spirit's imperishable promise seals us. The Spirit of Christ guarantees our inheritance until the day of redemption. We will be transformed from bodies that wrinkle and fail with age into glorified beings just like Jesus' glorified body. All those who hear, believe, and receive the word of truth—the gospel message of saving grace—are purchased and then sealed from God's just and righteous wrath. We are saved for that great day when we will be glorified and come into our eternal inheritance.[31]

But our citizenship is in heaven. And we eagerly await a Savior from there, the

---

24 Romans 6:23.
25 1 Corinthians 15:55.
26 1 Corinthians 15:57.
27 Romans 5:3—5.
28 Romans 5:5.
29 1 Corinthians 15:42—45.
30 1 Corinthians 15:49.
31 Ephesians 1:13—14.

Lord Jesus Christ, who, by the power that enables him to bring everything under his control, will transform our lowly bodies so that they will be like his glorious body. (Philippians 3:20–21)

Our great hope is for the fulfillment of the promise of salvation on the day of the Lord. Our Savior rose from the grave in resurrection power, and He is our hope. In Him we have an eternal assurance that all who fall asleep in the Lord will be called up "with a loud command, with the voice of the archangel and with the trumpet call of God." Those who are still living will be caught up together with those who rest in peace. We will meet the Lord in the air and then dwell with Him forever.[32]

Today, we can stand with Job in boundless hope and declare, "I know that my redeemer lives, and that in the end he will stand on the earth."[33] Our eternal hope assures us that when our flesh is destroyed, we will see God.[34]

Praise be to the God and Father of our Lord Jesus Christ! In his great mercy he has given us new birth into a living hope through the resurrection of Jesus Christ from the dead, and into an inheritance that can never perish, spoil or fade. This inheritance is kept in heaven for you, who through faith are shielded by God's power until the coming of the salvation that is ready to be revealed in the last time. (1 Peter 1:3–5)

Online maps offer alternate routes to your destination depending on traffic flows and road construction. But apps that offer alternative routes are not the way of God's kingdom. Our Lord and Savior gets rid of any confusion by making the way straight.[35] He offers one clear path to come to saving faith. The way is only by grace and through faith. We don't have to be tech savvy to find this path. Our Savior searches for us and gifts us with salvation in three parts to make it triple strong. A three-fold gift of God who lights the pathway before us.

When we are counted among the redeemed, it is the time for effort on our part. We're discipled in His church so we may grow in our faith and add goodness, knowledge, self-control, perseverance, godliness, and brotherly love to this great gift of saving grace. We must learn to obey, devote ourselves to Christ, deny ourselves and take up our cross, walk as Jesus' walked, do the work of our calling in God's kingdom, and join the grand cause of saving faith.

God's sons and daughters have a great confidence as they grow in faith and

---

32 1 Thessalonians 4:15—18.
33 Job 19:25.
34 Job 19:26.
35 Isaiah 40:3, Luke 3:6.

serve in the church. We have a sure hope, and perfect assurance that we will be raised up to see our Lord and God face to face. We look forward with certainty to the day of the Lord when we will know our heavenly Father as well as He knows us. Christ Jesus will be fully revealed as He brings us into the beautiful mysteries of the kingdom of heaven.

> After this I heard what sounded like the roar of a great multitude in heaven shouting: "Hallelujah Salvation and glory and power belong to our God. (Revelation 19:1)

Chapter 14 Q&A

The Essence of the Gospel

1. Why does salvation come in three parts?

_____

_____

_____

2. How are we justified and given peace with God?

_____

_____

_____

3. What is the dichotomy we face in sanctification?

_____

_____

_____

4. Describe sanctification's part in our salvation?

_____

_____

_____

5. When life's present troubles try to crush us, what hope do we have?

_____

_____

_____

My Journey's Journal:

Chapter 15: The Joy of His Salvation

Key Scriptures:

- "Create in me a pure heart, O God, and renew a steadfast spirit within me. Do not cast me from your presence or take your Holy Spirit from me. Restore to me the joy of your salvation and grant me a willing spirit, to sustain me" (Psalm 51:10–12).

- "But only the redeemed will walk there, and those the Lord has rescued will return. They will enter Zion with singing; everlasting joy will crown their heads. Gladness and joy will overtake them, and sorrow and sighing will flee away" (Isaiah 35:9–10).

When a child turns into a teen, they start to think about freedom from Dad and Mom's constant, caring watch. They dream about getting their own wheels so they can get out on their own and do the things they want. Their fantasies of freedom rarely include thoughts of the responsibility that come with it. After years of saving their allowance from mowing the lawn and raking leaves, they have enough cash to buy that old Ford Ranger pickup. Their dream is finally realized, or so they think.

When they get away from home, they mess up, get caught, must confess, face consequences, and then get restored to Mom and Dad's good graces. An impish, wandering teen who comes home safe is cause for the whole family to rejoice.

When Christ is revealed to our wandering souls, our hearts cry out in repentance for our great offenses against a holy God. We plead for mercy so that the Holy Spirit will not be taken from us. We pray for gracious forgiveness to restore us to the joy of God's salvation. Our hearts plead for a submitted spirit—an obedience that sustains us.

The psalmist offers a beautiful picture of turning our mourning into the oil of joy. He calls us to recognize our fallibilities. Even though we constantly trip and fall, God's Word reminds us that His abundant grace restores repentant hearts, wounded souls, and wandering spirits. As God's redeemed people, we can sing out with everlasting joy as we look forward to the day when sorrows will be no more, and gladness and joy will be ours forever.

> A prayer according to Isaiah 40:31:
>
> Oh, Lord Almighty, give us hearts that hope in you so that you may renew your strength in us. Give us wings to soar like the eagles. Be our strength so we may run and not grow weary. Give us feet to walk and not grow faint.

Ezekiel portrays a powerfully graphic picture of who we were when our heavenly Father found us and rescued us from cruel abandonment in this sin-bent world. He describes a discarded infant laying in an open field in her own blood. "'Then I passed by and saw you kicking about in your blood, and as you lay there in your blood I said to you, "Live!"'

Then when she grew up; "'Later I passed by, and when I looked at you and saw that you were old enough for love, I spread the corner of my garment over you and covered your naked body. I gave you my solemn oath and entered into a covenant with you," declares the Sovereign Lord, "and you became mine."

Then He prepared her to be His bride; "So you were adorned with gold and silver; your clothes were of fine linen and costly fabric and embroidered cloth. Your food was honey, olive oil and the finest flour. You became very beautiful and rose to be a queen."[1]

What incredible joy it is to be rescued as an abandoned child and then prepared as the bride of Christ. She is adorned with the precious jewels of God's kingdom—a bride prepared for His coming.[2]

I delight greatly in the Lord; my soul rejoices in my God. For he has clothed me with garments of salvation and arrayed me in a robe of his righteousness, as a bridegroom adorns his head like a priest, and as a bride adorns herself with her jewels. (Isaiah 61:10)

Those who are forgiven much overflow with love for their Redeemer.[3] He washes away our sin and filth, cleansing us with the blood of the Lamb who takes away the sins of the world.[4] The saints rise and pray, "Come, Lord Jesus, and sweep this land clean of our many transgressions. May our many sins be swept away. Come, our Redeemer, forgive us, cleanse us, make us whole, and fill our mouths with songs of exaltation before the Lord Almighty."

The earth we defile with our sin is set free from its bondage through repentance.[5] Then the angels in heaven shout out with jubilant songs because of what the Lord has done. When sins are forgiven, our heavenly Father sets the mountains, meadows, and forests free to burst into joyful songs and reveal the glory of God's creation.

1 Ezekiel 16:6—13.
2 Revelation 19:7.
3 Luke 7:47.
4 John 1:29.
5 Romans 8:21.

I have swept away your offenses like a cloud, your sins like the morning mist. Return to me, for I have redeemed you." Sing for joy, you heavens, for the Lord has done this; shout aloud, you earth beneath. Burst into song, you mountains, you forests and all your trees, for the Lord has redeemed Jacob, he displays his glory in Israel.
(Isaiah 44:22–23)

We were once captives to sin just as Israel was enslaved in Egypt. We cried out for mercy because of the chains of sin that bound us. The Lord heard our cry and saved us and delivered us with mighty acts and outstretched arm.[6]

Our sufferings, tests, and trials press in from every side, and we wash them in tears of grief and sorrow. When life's storms and calamities buffet us, we call out to the One who covers us in the shadow of His wings. We weep in sympathy for those who are afflicted. We offer compassionate help to those who are weak. In all our sorrows, we continue to sow the good seeds of God's Word and water them with our tears. We overcome all evil with good.

Look and rejoice! There's a joyful harvest springing up from the ground. Then we reap God's abundant blessings as we bring in the harvest. Our sorrowful sadness and our godly lamenting turn into reaping with the joyful exaltations of the redeemed.

Those who sow with tears will reap with songs of joy. Those who go out weeping, carrying seed to sow, will return with songs of joy, carrying sheaves with them.
(Psalm 126:5–6)

We may go shopping for new clothes because we feel down in the dumps. Our frumpy old sweater has holes in the elbows and snags on the arms. Our shoes have a thousand miles of road dirt and stains. Our pockets have holes, and our money is long gone. We feel ashamed. We've neglected things for too long.

But what if the store took our old clothes in even exchange for all the new outfits we need, including shoes and accessories? This is the way it is in the economy of God's kingdom. We come in filthy rags and go out as a bride adorned for her beloved.[7]

And provide for those who grieve in Zion–to bestow on them a crown of beauty instead of ashes, the oil of joy instead of mourning, and a garment of praise instead of a spirit of despair. They will be called oaks of righteousness, a planting of the Lord for the display of his splendor.
(Isaiah 61:3)

The joy of the Lord gives us strength to endure to the end when sorrowful weeping will be no more. The power of God's Word ministered to us by the Holy Spirit strengthens us in soul and spirit so that we may not be weary in well doing as we await with expectation for our Bridegroom. We hold fast to God's

6 Psalm 136:12.
7 Revelation 21:2.

promises, and they carry us through sufferings, hardships, distress, and troubles. Standing in God's counsel strengthens our faith. We keep our lamps filled with oil—trimmed and ready. There's a song in our heart as we prepare ourselves as a bride adorned for His coming. God's promises fill our hearts with expectation for the day we'll hear the shout: "Here's the bridegroom! Come out to meet him!"[8]

He will wipe every tear from their eyes. There will be no more death or mourning or crying or pain, for the old order of things has passed away. (Revelation 21:4)

People trapped in the dealings of darkness and those crushed under the weight of sin see a great hope when they call out for mercy to the Lord who is mighty to save. Our Lord Jesus reaches out His nail-scarred hands to lift lost souls out of the dregs of darkness. He sets their feet upon the Rock who is Christ. The Redeemer comes to lift spirits once crushed by transgressions. He wipes away tears shed in secret in the night hours. He gives life to those who are dead in their trespasses and sins.[9]

In a moment, a great light is revealed to people living in darkness. The light dawns for those caught in the shadow of death.[10] Those He calls out of sin's darkness, whose feet are planted on the Rock, rise with a joyful song, a harvest chorus, and victorious hymns of praise. The breath of the Spirit gives wind to songs from the heart so the redeemed may they sing out with joyous exaltations to the Lord of the harvest.

As for you, you were dead in your transgressions and sins, in which you used to live when you followed the ways of this world. But because of his great love for us, God, who is rich in mercy, made us alive with Christ even when we were dead in transgressions—it is by grace you have been saved. (Ephesians 1:1–2, 4–5)

---

8 Matthew 25:6.
9 Ephesians 2:1.
10 Matthew 4:16.

Chapter 15 Q&A

The Joy of the Harvest

1. What great work has God accomplished that makes all creation rejoice?

_____

_____

_____

2. What is the connection between sowing with tears and reaping with songs of joy?

_____

_____

_____

3. Describe the way the economy works in God's kingdom?

_____

_____

_____

4. Why does Christ's bride in waiting overflow with songs of joy and praise?

_____

_____

_____

My Journey's Journal:

Part IV

Clothed with Power

"You are witnesses of these things. I am going to send you what my Father has promised; but stay in the city until you have been clothed with power from on high."
(Luke 24:48–49)

Prayerful preparation is a vital part of sending ambassadors of Christ. They must be well taught so they can live in keeping with repentance, in agreement with their baptism, and with Jesus as Lord of their lives. This part of the study guide teaches students of the Word so they may know the powerful bond of fellowship they have in Christ that strengthens them in the work of their calling in an ever-expanding church.

Chapter 16: Called, Chosen, and Faithful

Key Scriptures:

- "For many are invited, but few are chosen" (Matthew 22:14).

- "They will wage war against the Lamb, but the Lamb will triumph over them because he is Lord of lords and King of kings—and with him will be his called, chosen and faithful followers" (Revelation 17:14).

If someone offered you a mansion on a hilltop, would you refuse to move in because of a fear of the unknown? Would the lurking shadows you see through the curtains fill you with fear? Then, what you see grows bigger, and the giants you imagine get larger, causing you to shrink back with anxious thoughts.

The people of Israel were God's called and chosen nation. But fear of giants and powerful nations kept them from entering the Promised Land. They wandered in the wilderness for forty years because they were fearful and not faithful. The generation that God delivered from Egypt could not enter the Promised Land "because of their unbelief."[1] The writer of Hebrews warns us not to follow in their path, lest Christ become "a stone of stumbling, and a rock of offence."[2] "Let us, therefore, make every effort to enter that rest, so that no one will perish by following Israel's example of disobedience."[3]

Jesus provided an atoning sacrifice for our sins, and for the sins of every person in the whole world. He does not want anyone to perish for their sins. Our Savior's desire is for "everyone to come to repentance." Yeshua, our Savior, provided the way for those who answer His call and join with the King of kings and Lord of lords in His victory. We are made overcomers in Christ so we may serve as His called, chosen, and faithful disciples.

> A prayer according to Isaiah 41:10:
>
> Our Lord God and Father, give us hearts that do not fear, knowing that you are ever present with us. Open our eyes to see that you are the Great I AM who strengthens us and helps us, and who upholds us with your righteous right hand.

Have you ever walked through the aisles of the grocery store, filled your shopping cart, put all your stuff on the checkout belt, and then realized you

1 Hebrews 3;18—19.
2 1 Peter 2:8.
3 Hebrews 4:11.

forgot your wallet? In God's kingdom, the spiritual food we need comes without cost. It's better than a prepaid grocery gift card.

Has the Spirit of grace given you a hunger for God's Word? Have the holy Scriptures given you a thirst for the fountain of life? Then answer Jesus' call to come into God's kingdom where His sons and daughters "feast on the abundance of your house." Come to abide in God's dwelling place where He leads His children to "drink from your river of delights."[4] The invitation is in your hands. By grace you are given ears to hear your heavenly Father's call. Come, and enter the joy of the Lord.

Come, all you who are thirsty, come to the waters; and you who have no money, come, buy and eat! Come, buy wine and milk without money and without cost. (Isaiah 55:1)

You know that are not saved by your own efforts. You understand that you are not called and chosen because of anything you have done or not done. You answered Jesus' call to believe and be baptized.[5] You are God's much-loved sons and daughters, called by His name.

Now, the love of Christ compels you to be faithful and live in keeping with repentance. Those who disciple us encourage us to make every effort to grow in grace and knowledge of our Lord and Savior Jesus Christ. The Scriptures compel us to live in agreement with our baptism. Searching God's Word and feasting on the Scriptures strengthens us so that we may overrule the flesh and remain faithful to our calling in Christ.

Consider Israel, God's chosen nation. The men were circumcised on the eighth day. They made pilgrimages to Jerusalem to worship during annual feasts. They observed the Day of Atonement. They were a nation called by God's holy name, but they lived like those who were never called by His name.[6] They turned sacred feasts into self-absorbed festivals.

Paul declared this truth, writing, "For not all who are descended from Israel are Israel."[7] They became complacent in their faith and saw God as insufficient. They rejected God as King and turned to other gods. They deceived themselves with a lie and their duplicity ended in chaos because "Israel had no king; everyone did as they saw fit."[8] Now in our day we must remember that we can't make our own way of salvation, come to saving faith by our own means, or by any path we choose.[9]

---

4 Psalm 36:8.
5 Mark 16:16.
6 Isaiah 63:19.
7 Romans 9:6.
8 Judges 17:6, 21:13.
9 Matthew 22:11—12.

Make every effort to enter through the narrow door, because many, I tell you, will try to enter and will not be able to.
(Luke 13:24)

Those who claim Jesus' name as their own but refuse Him as Lord of their lives walk a treacherous path. When people persist with unrepentant hearts and continually refuse to follow the gospel's commands, our Savior becomes a stumbling stone, a rock of offense to them. When people try to depend on their own righteousness to gain saving grace, they stumble on the Rock who is Jesus Christ. They may feel pious and religious because of their external Christian traditions and rituals, but they stumble because this was "what they were destined for."

God's called and chosen are compelled to remain faithful as His sons and daughters. His royal servant priests in His holy nation are called to bring honor to His holy name. All those who hear, believe, and receive the Good News that Jesus proclaimed are set free from sin's shackles. Those who were once spiritually blind now see. People who are in Christ are set free from sin's oppression, come into the Lord's favor, and receive mercy. Why would we not love Him who lavished His forgiveness on us? His boundless love is the impulse that keeps us faithfully abiding in Him and feasting at His table.

"A stone that causes people to stumble and a rock that makes them fall." They stumble because they disobey the message–which is also what they were destined for. But you are a chosen people, a royal priesthood, a holy nation, God's special posses- sion, that you may declare the praises of him who called you out of darkness into his wonderful light. Once you were not a people, but now you are the people of God; once you had not received mercy, but now you have received mercy.
(1 Peter 2:8–10)

Christians who run away when Jesus' calls have a whale of a problem. Because of His overwhelming love, He does not want any to perish. Remember that God is faithful even when we are not faithful. If necessary, He will send a giant fish to bring us back to walk on His narrow path. Then He cleanses us so we may faithfully serve.[10]

He prepared a job for every Christian according to His plan prepared in advance for each one.[11] If we wander off in another direction, our God is more than able to lead us back onto the right path. Each of God's sons and daughters serve a vital part in the work of the great commission, and our God remains faithful, and He will bring us back to complete this good work.

If you have wandered away from your calling in Christ, rejoice that your heavenly Father restores the years your sin has eaten.[12] He is longsuffering with

10 Hebrews 9:14.
11 Ephesians 2:10.
12 Joel 2:25.

you. He waits patiently and with longing for you to return from wallowing in the muck with the pigs.[13] His Holy Spirit continually pierces your wayward heart to convict of willful ways and bring you to your knees in repentance.

The Lord is not slow in keeping his promise, as some understand slowness. Instead he is patient with you, not wanting anyone to perish, but everyone to come to repentance. (2 Peter 3:9)

Remember the time you forgot all about eating lunch because you were so engrossed a fun project? When a job totally engages your heart and mind, that juicy apple and ham-and-cheese sandwich must wait. God's called, chosen, and faithful have the attitude of Christ, and the work of God's kingdom fully satisfies them. He strengthens you by the Word and the Spirit to remain faithful and complete the good work God has prepared for you.

Paul and Barnabas are great examples. They were "committed to the grace of God for the work." They gathered the church to rejoice with them because of the work they faithfully completed on their missionary journeys.[14]

"My food," said Jesus, "is to do the will of him who sent me and to finish his work." (John 4:34)

It's all free! It's a gift and you don't even have to unwrap it. Do you hear the voice of one who is calling in the wilderness, "prepare the way of the Lord?"[15] Hear the call to "come to the waters."[16] Your Redeemer has cleared the way, prepared a way, and by His grace opened your heart to answer the call. By His sacrificial work of the cross, Jesus made a way for you to come with repentant hearts and be made one with Christ who is victorious over sin, Satan, and death.

But His good work in you has just begun. We are overcomers in Christ and prepared as a bride by the power of the Word and the Holy Spirit. As you continue to learn from the holy Scriptures and grow in grace and knowledge of Jesus Christ, you are prepared to go out and echo Jesus' words to all those who thirst for the water of life, "Come."

The Spirit and the bride say, "Come!" And let the one who hears say, "Come!" Let the one who is thirsty come; and let the one who wishes take the free gift of the water of life. (Revelation 22:17)

A seed planted in the ground sprouts up through the soil to make a gardener's heart rejoice. But if that sprout isn't watered, it withers and dies. When we

---

13 Luke 15:15—16.
14 Acts 4:26—27.
15 Isaiah 40:3, Matthew 3:3.
16 Isaiah 55:1.

are brought to saving faith in Jesus Christ and baptized into the Father, Son, and Holy Spirit, we are like fresh, green sprouts in the garden of God—new creations in Christ.

Those who join in sweet fellowship with people of faith find a good place to grow in grace and knowledge. They need strength from God's Word and encouragement to feast on the inspired words of the apostles and prophets so they will grow and faithfully produce good fruit. But being a fine sprout is just a good beginning. We must grow to become strong in the faith and persevere so we may run the race set before us.[17] The champions of our faith cheer on God's called and chosen sons and daughters. Their example encourages us to feast on the holy Scriptures to be strengthened as faithful disciples of Jesus Christ.

> Let us run with endurance the race that is set before us, looking to Jesus, the founder and perfecter of our faith, who for the joy that was set before him endured the cross, despising the shame, and is seated at the right hand of the throne of God.
> (Hebrews 12:2 ESV)

Chapter 16 Q&A

Called, Chosen, and Faithful

1. What must God's sons and daughters do to remain true to their calling in Jesus Christ?

_____

_____

2. How does the Good News effect the lives of God's called and chosen people?

_____

_____

3. When Christians run away from our calling in Christ, what does our heavenly Father do?

_____

_____

4. Isn't being called and chosen enough? What does faithfulness have to do with being God's children?

_____

_____

17 Hebrews 12:1.

My Journey's Journal:

Chapter 17: A Sending Church

Key Scriptures:

- "While they were worshiping the Lord and fasting, the Holy Spirit said, 'Set apart for me Barnabas and Saul for the work to which I have called them.' So after they had fasted and prayed, they placed their hands on them and sent them off" (Acts 13:2–3).

- "And this gospel of the kingdom will be preached in the whole world as a testimony to all nations, and then the end will come" (Matthew 24:14).

Well-orchestrated beginning notes set the stage for a great crescendo that leads to an awesome finale. The way we begin the work of God's kingdom is an essential part of proclaiming our testimony of Jesus Christ to the nations. The church in Antioch offers a perfect example for a sending church—worship, fast, pray, listen to the Spirit, and then prayerfully lay hands on those who will be sent.

Apart from the Holy Spirit, the church has no oil to keep the eternal flame burning. Spiritual gifts the Spirit imparts in the fellowship of believers are vital because every person who goes home after worship is sent out as an ambassador of Christ—first to their neighbors, then to their community, and finally, those who are sent across borders to other nations. We all need the light of Christ to burn in our temples.[1]

> A prayer according to Matthew 28:19:
>
> Spirit of Life, anoint, gift, and empower your servants so we may go and make disciples, baptizing them into the name of the Father, Son, and Holy Spirit.

A room full of learners is no school without a teacher. Mission statements without a missionary are little more than an idea. How will people hear the Good News gospel of Jesus Christ unless someone is sent to call them out of sin's darkness into the light of life?

We live in a nation that has hidden the light of Christ from our children. Because of this, there's an invasive darkness spreading over the land. There are too few workers in the harvest field who are prepared in the church and then sent out to proclaim Christ and Him crucified.[2] There are not enough voices to proclaim that Jesus' sacrifice cleanses away sin.

1 1 Corinthians 6:19.
2 1 Corinthians 2:2.

The church must prepare and send Christ's ambassadors to proclaim the joy and blessings of the gospel. Jesus' followers call out to wandering souls, "Come to the Lord's bountiful table." Those who are sent out from the church lead lost souls to Christ, the One who came in the flesh to die in our place and for our sins. Look and you will see feet fastened with gospel shoes so beautiful as they go out to preach and proclaim our risen Savior.

How, then, can they call on the one they have not believed in? And how can they believe in the one of whom they have not heard? And how can they hear without someone preaching to them? And how can anyone preach unless they are sent? As it is written: "How beautiful are the feet of those who bring good news!"
(Romans 10:14–15)

The Spirit of God anointed a man named John and gave him a voice to call the people to repentance. He served as, "A voice of one calling in the wilderness, 'Prepare the way for the Lord, make straight paths for him.'"[3] He prepared the way for our Lord Jesus Christ to come and dwell among the people.

In this light, consider Malachi's prophetic oracle—the last words written in the Old Testament.

See, I will send the prophet Elijah to you before that great and dreadful day of the Lord comes. He will turn the hearts of the parents to their children, and the hearts of the children to their parents; or else I will come and strike the land with total destruction."
(Malachi 4:5–6)

The Father sent John to prepare the way for Immanuel who was born among men. Then a host of angels sang out to accompany Jesus' birth, "Glory to God in the highest heaven, and on earth peace to those on whom his favor rests."[4] Now, we, too, are called to go as witnesses. He puts His Word in our mouth to call people to repent and come and trust in Jesus with hearts that rejoice in His salvation.[5] Our Redeemer beckons us to proclaim the light of the world. Now we proclaim the Word so that people may hear and believe in Jesus Christ as Lord and Savior and prepare for His second coming.

There was a man sent from God whose name was John. He came as a witness to testify concerning that light, so that through him all might believe. He himself was not the light; he came only as a witness to the light.
(John 1:6–8)

The church sends us out to give testimony of Christ Jesus' good work in our lives. We received God's saving grace. His healing touch restores our wounded souls. We know Christ Jesus who came in the flesh and gave His body to be

3 Luke 3:4.
4 Luke 4:16.
5 Psalm 13:5.

broken to heal us in body, soul, and spirit. We have a Savior who was born of the virgin Mary, walked among us, and then gave His life blood for the forgiveness and cleansing of sin.

When we were baptized into the Father, Son, and Holy Spirit, we died with Christ, were buried with Christ, and then raised up in resurrection power with Christ. The triune God provides three sure witnesses of our salvation. Jesus offered His blood to be shed on our behalf. Then He gave us the waters of baptism and the Spirit who marks us with a seal.[6] Now we are ready for discipling and anointing before the church sends us to declare God's mighty works and give testimony of God's forgiveness and an abundance of saving grace.

> *This is how we know that we live in him and he in us: He has given us of his Spirit. And we have seen and testify that the Father has sent his Son to be the Savior of the world.*
> (John 4:13–14)

We have a mission field that's ripe for the harvest. Where do we find it? It is wherever there are people who have not heard God's promise of saving faith in Jesus Christ. That place can be the local coffee shop or in faraway Timbuktu. Your place to testify may be at the table where you feed your hungry children or in a rest home where you visit your aging parents and their friends.

At this point, it's worth noting that organized religion often creates obstacles to spreading the gospel message. A sending church must be organized, but missionary committees are seldom effective if they do not allow the Holy Spirit to lead the way in planning and implementing a missional work. Worship, fasting, earnest prayers, taking time to listen to the Spirit, and then laying on of hands to empower those who will be sent is more effective than planning sessions alone.

The power we need for this work does not come by means of our God-given common talents—not by horses, chariots, or strength of horsemen.[7] We don't find our spiritual gift for witnessing through mystical spiritual happenings. Gifts of the Spirit don't sneak up on us unawares. Spiritual gifts cannot be discovered. Written tests and assessment tools help us identify our God given common gifts but are not useful for imparting spiritual gifts. Ministry and service gifts are imparted only as the Spirit wills and often by laying on of hands.

By means of the empowering spiritual gifts of the Holy Spirit, we have the fire necessary for the impossible work of the great commission. As we take the Word of life and the means of grace to our next-door neighbor, we cannot be effective without the anointing and gifting work of the Spirit of Christ. The Spirit of grace empowers us to speak, and then He opens the ears of those to whom we witness as He wills.

---

6 Romans 5:9, Galatians 3:26—27, Romans 8:16—17.
7 Isaiah 31:1.

But you will receive power when the Holy Spirit comes on you; and you will be my witnesses in Jerusalem, and in all Judea and Samaria, and to the ends of the earth.
(Acts 1:8)

All of us have different gifts, talents, and special ways of communicating. Very few Christians can effectively proclaim the gospel in a bar or night club without imbibing in the overflow of liquid spirits. Not many of us can effectively speak before a crowd unless the Spirit first speaks to us and then emboldens us to open our mouths.[8]

Our purpose in witnessing is to open people's eyes to see their need of Christ, just as Jesus, the Word of Life, opened Zacchaeus' eyes. There's no doubt that when Jesus spoke to the tax collector, just a few words changed his heart. He saw his sin and turned from it, pledging to repay all those he had cheated. Now Jesus sends us in the authority of His name and in the power of the Holy Spirit to seek out those who are bound in the chains of their sin.

But Zacchaeus stood up and said to the Lord, "Look, Lord! Here and now I give half of my possessions to the poor, and if I have cheated anybody out of anything, I will pay back four times the amount." Jesus said to him, "Today salvation has come to this house, because this man, too, is a son of Abraham. For the Son of Man came to seek and to save the lost."
(Luke 19:8–10)

It's dangerous for us to be sent out in our own strength, with our own words, and according to our own plan.[9] If we try, we may end up naked and wounded.[10] We must first be hearers of God's Word, then we can be doers of the word.[11] As ambassadors of Christ, we have no words of our own to speak. We speak what we hear the Spirit speaking. He knows the hearts of those to whom we witness, and He knows the words that reveal a Savior who turns their hearts to hear and receive His saving grace. These are the words we speak out as representatives of Christ and the cross to proclaim Jesus' death until He comes.

We are therefore Christ's ambassadors, as though God were making his appeal through us.
(2 Corinthians 5:20)

Most countries send ambassadors to represent the nation with the full backing of their government. In the same way, we are sent as witnesses to go in the power and authority of God's holy name to represent His kingdom. Our church, friends, and family have a vital part in sending the gospel's envoys. When we witness over the backyard fence to our neighbor, we need fervent prayers to back

8 Ezekiel 3:27.
9 Psalm 127:1, Isaiah 8:10, Acts 5:38.
10 Acts 19:13—16.
11 James 1:22.

118

us up. Those who are called to raise Christ's banner in Sudan need God's armor and an abundance of prayers, support, and encouragement.

Prayer opens barred doors. Intercessions of the saints lift us up from the deepest valleys, crush mountain sized obstacles, smooth out the rough spots in the road, and level the rugged places at every turn so that the Lord may reveal His glory to all who will see.[12] Prayers of the saints strengthen us and keep us from giving in to pressure and compromising the truth because we're afraid of the crowd.[13]

Devote yourselves to prayer, being watchful and thankful. And pray for us, too, that God may open a door for our message, so that we may proclaim the mystery of Christ, for which I am in chains. Pray that I may proclaim it clearly, as I should.
(Colossians 4:2–4)

When it comes to testifying, we must know who we are in Christ. If we don't know that we are sent in the power and authority of His name, we have no confidence. Without knowledge of Christ who indwells us, we have no impulse or purpose. We must be confident of the Spirit of Christ who indwells us so we may boldly proclaim the mystery of the gospel.

How does Christ's indwelling presence affect our life? Our Savior leads us to serve as a called, chosen, and faithful people. We are much loved sons and daughters of the Most High God. Christians bear the name of Christ as their family name. He gives the authority of His name to His disciples who minister and serve. Christ Jesus called us to minister as royal priests in His kingdom and under authority. In Christ we are in covenant with our heavenly Father and prepared to declare the praises of His mighty works everywhere we are sent. He brought us out of the world's darkness so that we may walk in the light of Christ and bear witness to the light.

But you are a chosen people, a royal priesthood, a holy nation, God's special posses-sion, that you may declare the praises of him who called you out of darkness into his wonderful light.
(1 Peter 2:9)

When a congregation is led into true worship, they turn into a sending church. Gatherings of the faithful constantly send people out to testify. They come together and take time to fast in the Lord s presence. Every house of prayer disciples their people and sends them to neighbors, coworkers, and to the na-

---

12 Isaiah 40:4—5.
13 1 Samuel 15:24, Matthew 21:26.

tions as witnesses of Christ and the cross. A gathering of the faithful takes time to listen and hear God's Word and then do what it says. They are powerfully equipped and prepared to be sent out ambassadors to represent the kingdom of heaven. A local Christian assembly lays hands on workers to impart the empowering work of the Spirit for the power and authority necessary for the missional work set before them.

A sending congregation knows that the power to do the work of the Great Commission does not come by means of God-given common talents. A church that is focused on proclaiming the gospel to the nations knows the work is impossible by their own means. They come together and prayerfully lay hands on those who will minister and serve to send them in the power, strength, and anointing of the Spirit of Christ.

> Pray also for me, that whenever I speak, words may be given me so that I will fearlessly make known the mystery of the gospel. (Ephesians 6:19)

Chapter 17 Q&A

A Sending Church

1. Describe the beauty of feet that put on gospel shoes.

_____

_____

2. If people are sent to serve in their own strength, what can be accomplished?

_____

_____

3. What mighty work does God do in our lives as He prepares us to serve as witnesses?

_____

_____

4. What is the best way for a church to plan and implement a missional work?

_____

_____

5. How is a person given their spiritual gift so they may serve accordingly?

_____

_____

My Journey's Journal:

Chapter 18: Witnesses of Our Salvation

Key Scriptures:

- "Every matter must be established by the testimony of two or three witnesses" (2 Corinthians 13:1).

- "This is the one who came by water and blood—Jesus Christ. He did not come by water only, but by water and blood. And it is the Spirit who testifies, because the Spirit is the truth. For there are three that testify: the Spirit, the water and the blood; and the three are in agreement" (1 John 5:6–8).

Reliable witnesses are necessary to prove guilt or innocence in courts of justice. Circumstantial evidence should not be sufficient to verify what occurred. One testimony is not enough proof to establish that something did or did not occur. The gospel's writers offer three sure eyewitnesses of Jesus who came in the flesh, born of the virgin Mary, walked among us to teach, heal, and proclaim God's kingdom, and then offered Himself as the perfect Lamb of God to die in our place and for the sins of the world.

Baptism in water, Jesus' redemptive blood shed on the cross, and the Holy Spirit's witness are sure proof that Jesus is the Christ, the Son of the Living God, and our Savior. These three witnesses now serve as a sure testimony that Christ has saved us. We are justified by His blood, baptized into Christ by water and the Word, and sealed by the Holy Spirit. The Holy Spirit perfects the good work of saving grace and gives witness in our spirit to confirm that we are God's children.

> A prayer according to Romans 8:16–17:
>
> Spirit of Christ, may our soul and spirit embrace the Three in One who bears witness that we are adopted children of our heavenly Father and coheirs with Christ.

A worship gathering may heartily sing that great old hymn of the church, "Would you be free from the burden of sin? There's pow'r in the blood, pow'r in the blood." Then the congregation rings out with the refrain, "There is pow'r, pow'r, wonder-working pow'r. In the blood of the Lamb."[1]

Our heavenly Father sent His only Son, who was born in the flesh, to offer His life blood as a sacrifice for the sins of the world. All those whom the Spirit leads to saving faith are brought into this cleansing flow. The flow of blood from

---

1 Author: Lewis E. Jones. (1899) Public domain.

the nails driven into His hands and feet is still powerfully effective to justify, saving all those who hear and believe. They are sealed against God's just and righteous wrath and given right standing before the Father.

Since we have now been justified by his blood, how much more shall we be saved from God's wrath through him!
(Romans 5:9)

By grace and through faith in Jesus Christ, our heavenly Father adopts us as sons and daughters. We are His children—free from bondage to sin. The water and blood that flowed from Jesus' side made us God's called, chosen, and adopted sons and daughters. In the waters of baptism our flesh dies, we are buried, and then raised up in resurrection power with Christ. Indeed, we put on Christ our Savior. He wraps us in His robe of righteousness and leads us into God's holy presence.

So in Christ Jesus you are all children of God through faith, for all of you who were baptized into Christ have clothed yourselves with Christ.
(Galatians 3:26–27)

The third sure witness of our salvation is the Holy Spirit. He is the One Jesus promised to send as Comforter (John 14:16), as an Advocate (John 16:7), and as the Spirit of truth (John 15:26). The Holy Spirit teaches us all things and reminds us of all that Jesus taught.[2] The Spirit of grace gives testimony in our spirit that we are God's children.[3]

Jesus' indwelling presence is a powerful confirmation of saving faith. The Spirit of Christ actively works in our lives. He indwells our temple to comfort, teach, and intercede for us. The Holy Spirit's anointing, gifting, and empowering work in our lives prepares us for ministry. When we minister and serve in the power of the Spirit of grace, and this is an undeniable testimony of His power and might to save. The Spirit of wisdom and understanding, the Spirit of counsel and might, and the Spirit of the knowledge and the fear of the Lord are actively present in our lives to give testimony of God's saving faith at work in us.

And you also were included in Christ when you heard the message of truth, the gospel of your salvation. When you believed, you were marked in him with a seal, the promised Holy Spirit.
(Ephesians 1:13)

Now consider additional evidence of an active faith in Jesus Christ. The Holy Spirit gives us assurance that we are God's sons and daughters with an awesome inheritance. He lights a fire in us so we may serve and minister, proclaiming God's kingdom that dwells within us.[4]

When we suffer for the cross, this is a sure testimony of Christ's living and

---

2 John 14:26.
3 Romans 8:16.
4 Luke 17:21.

active presence at work in and through us. We can stand with the apostle Paul who rejoiced in suffering for the cross. He wrote to the church, "I fill up in my flesh what is still lacking in regard to Christ's afflictions."[5]

Is there anything lacking in Christ's sufferings? We must suffer for the cross until the work of His church is finished, and that work is not yet complete. Perseverance even in sufferings serve to advance the gospel message and offers a sure sign of Christ in us.[6]

> *The Spirit himself testifies with our spirit that we are God's children. Now if we are children, then we are heirs—heirs of God and co-heirs with Christ, if indeed we share in his sufferings in order that we may also share in his glory.*
> (Romans 8:16–17)

Hunger is a sure sign of life. Newborn puppies snuggle up to Momma to get their first taste of milk very soon after they're born. Having an appetite for God's Word and a desire to grow in grace and knowledge is evidence of a growing faith. Without this hunger, we will fail to thrive as born-again sons and daughters.

> *We ought always to thank God for you, brothers and sisters, and rightly so, because your faith is growing more and more, and the love all of you have for one another is increasing. Therefore, among God's churches we boast about your perseverance and faith in all the persecutions and trials you are enduring.*
> (2 Thessalonians 1:3–4)

Obeying the Father, Son, and Holy Spirit provides a witness of our union with Christ. Keeping the gospel's commands is proof that the Word is applied to our daily lives. If we claim to know God and His Son but don't walk according to truth, the truth is not in us. How can the love of Christ be made complete in us if we don't obey God's Word? If we claim Jesus as Savior, we must also make Him Lord of our lives.

When our Redeemer reigns supreme over our lives, love rules above all else.[7] Loving our brothers and sisters in Christ with the love of Christ is sure evidence that we walk in the light of the Son.[8]

> *To God's elect, exiles scattered throughout the provinces of Pontus, Galatia, Cappadocia, Asia and Bithynia who have been chosen according to the foreknowledge of God the Father, through the sanctifying work of the Spirit, to be obedient to Jesus Christ and sprinkled with his blood: Grace and peace be yours in abundance.*
> (1 Peter 1:1–2)

There is no greater gift than love. There is no greater service to our friends, neighbors, and our brothers and sisters in Christ than to love them as Christ

5 Colossians 1:24.
6 Philippians 1:12—14.
7 1 Corinthians 13:13.
8 1 John 2:3—9, John 8:12.

loved us. There is no greater ministry than to minister to those in need with the love of Christ. When we apply God's Word to our hearts, He changes our heart and our minds so that we may overflow with His love. We love our wives as Christ loved the church because He first loved us and betrothed us as His bride.

God's love shown toward us is a powerful witness of His saving grace at work in our lives. He gives us hearts that delight in the Him. He clothes us with garments of salvation. We are arrayed in a robe of His righteousness and adorned with the precious jewels of His kingdom.[9]

"A new command I give you: Love one another. As I have loved you, so you must love one another. By this everyone will know that you are my disciples, if you love one another." (John 13:34–35)

God set in place a foundational principle that everything is established by two or three witnesses.[10] With this truth in mind, consider that our heavenly Father sent His only Son, the Word of creation, to be born in the flesh. He came as Immanuel, Yeshua HaMashiach, conceived by the Holy Spirit in the virgin Mary and born among us. He walked the dusty roads of Galilee and Judea, offering signs and wonders to reveal Himself as fully God and fully man who is more than able to save.

At the very moment John baptized Jesus, the heavens opened, and the Holy Spirit descended upon Him like a dove. Then a voice from heaven gave witness, saying, "This is my Son, whom I love; with him I am well pleased."

Now the Father, Son, and Holy Spirit agree as one to give witness of our salvation. The three are in full agreement. They offer sure evidence as a testimony of God's saving grace at work in our lives. The Word of creation came among us by water and blood. He did not come by water only, but by water and blood.

We treasure heaven's testimony that constantly reassures us of our redemption through Jesus Christ. Then we see further evidence in our everyday lives that produce good fruit that comes from being grafted into the Vine, who is our Lord and Savior. The most beautiful proof is the love of Christ that overflows from us like a fountain to affect every person whose lives we touch.

Blessed are those who hunger and thirst for righteousness, for they will be filled. (Matthew 5:6)

9 Isaiah 61:10.
10 Deuteronomy 19:15, Matthew 18:16.

Chapter 18 Q&A

Witnesses of Our Salvation

1. How are Christians sealed and protected from God's just and righteous wrath?

_____

_____

_____

2. What three witnesses are offered to assure us that we are God's redeemed?

_____

_____

_____

3. How does the Holy Spirit give witness of our salvation?

_____

_____

_____

4. What additional evidence do we have as assurance that we are the redeemed sons and daughters of the Great I AM?

_____

_____

_____

My Journey's Journal:

Chapter 19: Enlarge the Place of Your Tent

Key Scriptures:

- "Enlarge the place of your tent, stretch your tent curtains wide, do not hold back; lengthen your cords, strengthen your stakes. For you will spread out to the right and to the left; your descendants will dispossess nations and settle in their desolate cities" (Isaiah 54:2–3).

- "Again he said, 'What shall we say the kingdom of God is like, or what parable shall we use to describe it? It is like a mustard seed, which is the smallest of all seeds on earth. Yet when planted, it grows and becomes the largest of all garden plants, with such big branches that the birds can perch in its shade'" (Mark 4:30–32).

There is a guiding principle in God's kingdom that shapes our vision for the church. The weak are made strong. Too little turns into more than enough.[1] God's plan to fill and subdue the earth began with one man, Adam, and his wife, Eve. The seed of Abraham was a small beginning in Yahweh's plan to provide a Redeemer, the Messiah, to save a people from being enslaved to sin.

Consider this truth. What people see as God's foolish plan of salvation is wiser than all collective human wisdom. The weakness of the cross is greater than all human strength put together.[2] The apostle Paul boasted of his weakness, knowing that God's power is best manifested in weak vessels.

This principle holds true for the once-barren woman who had no children but then bursts out in songs of joy because her house is bursting at the seams with many offspring. The glory of the Father raised His only Son from the grave in resurrection power to serve as Head of an ever-expanding church.[3]

Now He molds and shapes His called, chosen, and much-loved sons and daughters into a royal priesthood, a holy nation that serves to grow His family. The church must constantly spread out her tent curtains to make room for more. God's family of faith began small and humble, but now grows to be the largest in the garden.[4]

---

1 1 Kings 17:16.
2 1 Corinthians 1:25.
3 Romans 6:4, Colossians 1:18.
4 Matthew 13:31—32.

> A prayer according to Isaiah 9:3 and 1 Peter 2:9:
>
> God Almighty, enlarge your holy nation and increase our joy as those who rejoice at the harvest, and as warriors when dividing plunder.

God instructed the man and woman He created to fill the earth with off-spring.[5] But not just any children. We must fill the earth with children who belong to God and are called by His holy name.[6] We fail to fulfill God's covenant when we don't teach our children or lead them to be godly offspring. The earth can only be "subdued" when we send sons and daughters into the world to shine out with the light of Christ. Raising kids as environmentalists but apart from Christ will not fix an earth defiled and polluted by sin.[7] As an example, the kindest acts of those who look after our wildlife are of no account, unlike the godly who truly care for the needs of the animals.[8]

Adam and Eve yielded to Satan's deception, and the earth was no longer subject to them. The work of the second Adam restores what God established.[9] Our Lord Jesus paid the price for all sin so that, once again, all things may be under His feet.

Jesus came to be born in the flesh, a child laid down to sleep in a lowly cow trough. Then by the victory of the cross, He is "crowned with glory and honor because He came as a man and suffered death so that by the grace of God He might taste death for everyone."[10] He defeated death and now all things are made subject to Him and to all who are in Christ and called by His holy name.[11]

God blessed them and said to them, "Be fruitful and increase in number; fill the earth and subdue it. Rule over the fish in the sea and the birds in the sky and over every living creature that moves on the ground."
(Genesis 1:28)

A wife who could not have children is now an expectant mother. She prepares the nursery for a daughter with classic pink accents and bold floral wallpaper. She celebrates with her friends and family at a baby shower in her honor. The child in her womb is cause for singing. Grandma's heart overflows with joy.

But this is just a good beginning of training up a child in the Lord to prepare her for a life of leading many more souls into God's kingdom. One child raised, nurtured, and lovingly admonished in the Lord serves as a fruitful vine to produce a great harvest of souls.

But sadly, too many of us did not dedicate ourselves to teaching and training our children from birth. Now what do we do? Begin today! No matter if your

5 Genesis 1:28.
6 Malachi 2:15.
7 Isaiah 24:5.
8 Proverb s 12:10.
9 Hebrews 2:8.
10 Hebrews 2:9.
11 1 Corinthians 15:28.

child is five, sixteen, or forty. Begin right where you are now. Prayerfully equip yourself to be fruitful and then gently, lovingly serve to train your children to do their part in God's kingdom. Before long, your house will be bursting at the seams with many more of God's children.

> *"Sing, barren woman, you who never bore a child; burst into song, shout for joy, you who were never in labor; because more are the children of the desolate woman than of her who has a husband," says the Lord.*
> (Isaiah 54:1)

All families begin small. It begins with one man who loves one woman and then enters a covenant of marriage with her. This is a small but excellent start toward building a family of faith. Don't despair with modest starts. Take one day at a time to prepare yourself and then build a family with children who will be sent out and fill and subdue the earth in Jesus' holy name.

Who will despise such small beginnings?[12] One man, Abram, left home as a wayfarer on his way to a land he didn't know. His wife, Sarah, felt shamed because she was barren. Now Abraham is the father of countless people of faith. Small and impossible beginnings are the way of God's kingdom. The stump of Jesse was cut down, but then sprouted to become the branch that bears abundant fruit.[13] Jesus is the small stone cut out of a mountain, but not by the hands of a man. He is now the Capstone that fills the whole earth.[14]

Zerubbabel was only one man standing in the ruins of Jerusalem and its temple. But God called him to be strong. As one man, he faced an impossible task. Only the strength and power of the Spirit could accomplish this work. By the authority of God's holy name given to him as a signet he began by picking up one stone to lay a foundation.[15]

> *"Who dares despise the day of small things, since the seven eyes of the Lord that range throughout the earth will rejoice when they see the chosen capstone in the hand of Zerubbabel?*
> (Zechariah 4:10)

There you are, sitting on a rock in the blazing midday sun. You're in a barren wilderness that offers no shade. You're so parched you can't even shed tears. But our God and Father makes this desert valley a place of springs and covers it with pools.[16] Your valley of weeping turns into an oasis of blessing. Your Rock is Christ Jesus, where you stand to watch the desert blossom.

A small tent for two is soon too small. We must expand the tent and stake our tent pegs further out. The family grows and spreads out to the right and to the

12 Zechariah 4:10.
13 Isaiah 11:1.
14 Daniel 2:35.
15 Haggai 2:4, 23.
16 Psalm 84:6.

left. One small seed of faith blossoms into a holy nation—the church. Blessings overflow from this tent to those whom God has given His great and precious promises so they may participate in His divine nature.[17]

> *Therefore, "they are before the throne of God and serve him day and night in his temple; and he who sits on the throne will shelter them with his presence. 'Never again will they hunger; never again will they thirst. The sun will not beat down on them,' nor any scorching heat. For the Lamb at the center of the throne will be their shepherd; 'he will lead them to springs of living water.' 'And God will wipe away every tear from their eyes.'*
> (Revelation 7:15–17)

One little seed grows into a towering cedar tree that spreads more good seed to become a forest. A little spark flares up into a wildfire that turns thousands of acres of forest and meadows to ashes. Building a city skyscraper starts with the mayor digging one little shovel of dirt. Building strength to do a hundred repetitions starts with one shaky, agonizing pushup. God established the principle of small beginnings when He created one man, Adam.

Now in Christ, the power of the Spirit of Jesus makes even the weakest of us strong to be sent to proclaim the Good News. We're just one person doing our part. We spread the seed of the gospel that reveals Christ to those who are dead in their sins.

The good seeds of saving grace then produce more good seed. The revelation of God's Word brings many lost souls into the "tent," making it necessary to spread our tent curtains wide to welcome even more of God's sons and daughters into fellowship with the Son. The church, once like a barren bride, becomes the mother of many who grow the family of God.

Your people will rebuild the ancient ruins and will raise up the age-old foundations; you will be called Repairer of Broken Walls, Restorer of Streets with Dwellings. (Isaiah 58:12)

---

17 2 Peter 1:4.

Chapter 19 Q&A

Enlarge the Place of Your Tent

1. What does the Creator's command, "fill the earth and subdue it," call us to do?

_____

_____

_____

2. If we failed to start raising our children in a way that prepares them to subdue the earth, what can we do now?

_____

_____

_____

3. Why is the church likened to a tent with canopies, cords, and tent stakes?

_____

_____

_____

4. How is the church like a once barren widow whose house fills with many children?

_____

_____

_____

My Journey's Journal:

Chapter 20:
One With the Father, Son, and Holy Spirit

Key Scriptures:

- "He called you to this through our gospel, that you might share in the glory of our LORD Jesus Christ." (2 Thessalonians 2:14)

- "Make every effort to keep the unity of the Spirit through the bond of peace. There is one body and one Spirit, just as you were called to one hope when you were called; one LORD, one faith, one baptism, one God and Father of all, who is over all and through all and in all."

One pillar cannot support the whole building. We learn from wisdom who builds her house on seven pillars.[1] By wisdom, Jesus prepared James, Peter, and John to serve as pillars of the church.[2] A whole congregation is strengthened in the Spirit as they are joined together in a bond of peace to serve as pillars. We have one church, one Spirit, one Savior, one Father, one baptism, and one faith. They're all built together like many building stones in one house.

Some churches teach that God's salvation is not about us. But this teaching is a misguided form of false humility that comes from not knowing Christ who indwells us. The Lord Almighty gathers a remnant of people from every tribe, nation, and language on earth and makes us a holy nation. He adopts us as sons and daughters and gives us a new name so that we may exalt His holy name.[3]

Miles and borders may distance us, but when we are baptized into the name of the Father, Son, and Holy Spirit, we are built together as one. God's loving arms bring us together in a bond of love under one name—a family that brings glory to His holy name in all the earth.

> A prayer according to Ephesians 4:13:
>
> Lord Jesus, unite us in the faith according to the knowledge of the Son of God so we may become mature and attain the whole measure, the fullness of Christ.

You're included. You hear God's Word, and hearing the Word reveals Christ to you, and the seed of faith is planted in your heart. Those who believe the

---

1 Proverbs 9:1.
2 Galatians 2:9.
3 Psalm 29:2.

testimony of faithful witnesses come to saving faith. Our heavenly Father adopts us and gives us His name as our own and joins us to a family of fellowship. We're bound together, like being woven into one fine fabric.

What does it mean to be one with a holy God? It means that His glory is our glory.[4] Our Father feels our pain and our sorrows.[5] He hears and answers our prayers.[6] We are brought into a bond of fellowship that rejoices when we rejoice, hurts when we hurt, and grieves when we grieve.

On the day he comes to be glorified in his holy people and to be marveled at among all those who have believed. This includes you, because you believed our testimony to you. (2 Thessalonians 1:10)

God's glory is all encompassing. His kingdom is like an aegis that showers down with God's glory and the abundance of His kingdom upon all who are covered by it. Under this umbrella, Jesus is Lord of our lives. All those who are called by His name ought to glorify His holy name so that His name is glorified in us. The showers of blessing are possible because of the splendor of God's grace at work in our hearts and lives.

When Jesus is not Lord of our lives, we do whatever is right in our own eyes and bring dishonor upon God's holy name. When God's name is dishonored, we are dishonored. When the reputation of the church is tainted, all people who are the church are discredited. But when we honor and glorify God's holy name in our lives and in true worship, we bask in His glory.

We pray this so that the name of our Lord Jesus may be glorified in you, and you in him, according to the grace of our God and the Lord Jesus Christ. (2 Thessalonians 1:12)

How is it possible to comprehend the awesome beauty of being one with our heavenly Father? We come into fulfillment of this oneness when Christ returns for us. But even now as we walk earth's trodden pathways, we enjoy a oneness with the Lord Almighty who indwells us by the Holy Spirit. This unity is like a son who wears his hat just like Dad. He talks like Papa. He puts his thumbs in his pockets and stands tall and confident just like Daddy.

We are called to follow the example of godly leaders who walk as Jesus walked.[7] We're awash with God's Word, and the Scriptures season every word we speak. Some may protest, "Come on! I live in the real world." But even now in our everyday world, we are called to be one with Christ and give up our own ways and walk as Jesus walked.

---

4 John 17:22.
5 Psalm 103:13—14, Hebrews 4:15.
6 Psalm 91:15.
7 1 Corinthians 11:1.

On that day you will realize that I am in my Father, and you are in me, and I am in you.
(John 14:20)

The Scriptures admonish to abide in, to dwell in, and to partake of Christ. Partaking of the abundance of the Lord's Table unites us with our Savior and Lord. Receiving the bread and the cup unites us with our Redeemer and His body, the church. When we feast at the Lord's Table, our selfish ambitions become like dust that blows away. We are united in love, and by this love we will be known as a people who are called by God's holy name.[8] The love of Christ, who loved us first, unites us. This love reveals Christ to a lost world.

I in them and you in me–so that they may be brought to complete unity. Then the world will know that you sent me and have loved them even as you have loved me.
(John 17:23)

We live in a world polluted by sin and corrupted by those who live in rebellion against God who created us. Too many people defile the earth by spewing out curses with every sentence.[9] But a church with the mind of Christ speaks what He is speaking. We minister, serve, and worship with the heart and attitude of Christ, and our Savior is revealed to people who get caught up in the world's depravity. We raise a banner for people who are ensnared by sin's trap.

The church lives in the comfort of Christ's love and speaks out with His words of saving grace to lost souls. We who share in Christ's sufferings, persevere in our faith, grow in character, and rise in hope because God's love is poured into our hearts through the Holy Spirit who is given to us.[10] This is the church that puts on gospel shoes and effectively proclaims the Good News to wandering souls so they, too, may be united with Christ.

Therefore if you have any encouragement from being united with Christ, if any comfort from his love, if any common sharing in the Spirit, if any tenderness and compassion, then make my joy complete by being like-minded, having the same love, being one in spirit and of one mind.
(Philippians 2:1–2)

Our heavenly Father has begun a good work in us, and He is more than able to complete the work because He is faithful. Through His only Son, He brings us into the sweetest and most intimate fellowship ever known. Our Savior is the Good Shepherd who holds us close to His heart so that we may overcome the world's corrupting influence and temptations of the flesh. He longs to gather us like a hen gathers her chicks.[11] He covers us in the shadow of His wings with tender, loving care. He is our shield that extinguishes the enemy's fiery darts.[12]

---

8 1 John 13:35.
9 Isaiah 24:5.
10 Romans 5:3—5.
11 Luke 13:34.
12 Ephesians 6:16.

Through repentance and forgiveness, He keeps us blameless until the day of the Lord.[13] His abundant and free grace envelops us in close fellowship in His church. Because of His faithfulness and love for us, He holds us close and keeps us in fellowship. God's amazing love makes it clear that His great salvation is intimate and interpersonal.

He will also keep you firm to the end, so that you will be blameless on the day of our Lord Jesus Christ. God is faithful, who has called you into fellowship with his Son, Jesus Christ our Lord.
(1 Corinthians 1:8–9)

Consider the relational interactions between God's people and His mighty acts of justice. Lot lamented over the rampant, violent sin that pressed in all around him.[14] God heard his pleas and sent His servants to destroy Sodom and Gomorrah. But first the Lord came to tell Abraham what He was about to do.[15] The Lord listened to His friend as he plead on behalf of fifty, forty-five, thirty, twenty, and finally ten righteous people living in the towns of the Jordan valley.

Yahweh heard Abraham's plea and rescued Lot and his two daughters before destroying the cities because of the outcry against the rampant depravity and violence.

In our day, it's vital to understand our close relationship with the Father, Son, and Holy Spirit. Our God hears our cry against a world steeped in darkness and wanton immorality. He acts with just and righteous judgments against all who press in against us, intending to draw us into their blatant corruptions.

I no longer call you servants, because a servant does not know his master's business. Instead, I have called you friends, for everything that I learned from my Father I have made known to you.
(John 15:15)

We live in a spiritually dry and thirsty land. There's a famine of hearing God's Word.[16] Are the holy Scriptures taught, preached, and believed in every Christian church today? Our heavenly Father's eyes watch over those He calls "my people." He calls us "chosen." Our God remembers that He formed us for Himself with a great purpose—to proclaim His praises. We, the church, have not been faithful. But take heart because our heavenly Father remains faithful even when we are not. The gates of hell will not prevail against the church.[17]

Jesus, our High Priest, gathers us to worship, serve, and minister in His presence. We sing His praises every day as we look forward to gathering to worship as a congregation. The church serves to disciple and prepare people to send as <u>ambassadors so</u> they can go to their neighbors and to every island and continent

13 1 Thessalonians 5:23.
14 Genesis 19:7.
15 Genesis 18:17—19.
16 Amos 8:11—13.
17 Matthew 16:18.

138

on earth to proclaim God's praises. We declare what God has done to provide refreshing springs in a sun-scorched wilderness.

I provide water in the wilderness and streams in the wasteland, to give drink to my people, my chosen, the people I formed for myself that they may proclaim my praise. (Isaiah 43:20–21)

In God's kingdom, love reigns supreme. If the most spiritually gifted congregation has no love, they have failed to minister Christ and the cross. Godly love is the bonding agent that keeps a church from splintering into divisiveness and selfish ambitions. We enjoy a bond of fellowship in the Father's love, the ministry of Christ our High Priest, and the Holy Spirit who is our Comforter, Advocate, and Helper. But apart from the fullness of the triune God, the flame of a church becomes like a candle that goes out with a puff of smoke that blows away with the wind.[18] Without the love of Christ intimately at work in and through us, we have a false savior of our own design that is no more than wind and confusion.[19] A church without God's love is filled with nothing but noisemakers.[20]

The unifying power of Christ's love is like the breastplate that Israel's high priest wore on his chest when serving in the temple. Twelve precious stones adorned this priestly garment, each with the name of a tribe engraved on it. Jewels in settings of gold adorned the breastplate he wore close to his heart. Strands of blue, purple, and scarlet threads fashioned the wool fabric, interwoven with strands of gold. This beautifully crafted fabric was woven together to be strong, durable, and lasting—a perfectly beautiful display of the flawless unity of love the Father, Son, and Holy Spirit have for His sons and daughters.

And over all these virtues put on love, which binds them all together in perfect unity. (Colossians 3:14)

God calls us His friends. He befriends us and draws us into a family relationship with Him. Without this close-knit bond, we are like a button hanging by a thread—soon lost. But Christ weaves us together as many threads that make a strong and sure union. We are bound together with the one triune God. The bond of love we have in Christ enlightens us so we may delight to be one, in fellowship with our heavenly Father, the Son, and the Holy Spirit. This unbreakable union is possible because we are united with Christ through whom we "Received an inheritance from God, for he chose us in advance, and he makes

18 Psalm 68:2.
19 Isaiah 41:29.
20 1 Corinthians 13:1.

everything work out according to his plan."[21] God's saving grace brings us into a family and joins us together in love. This is a reciprocal love that encompasses all who are called by God's holy name.

> Even now my witness is in heaven; my advocate is on high. My intercessor is my friend as my eyes pour out tears to God. (Job 16:19–20)

Chapter 20 Q&A

One with the Father, Son, and Holy Spirit

1. How does our union with God affect our daily lives?

_____

_____

_____

2. What does it mean to have Jesus as Lord of your life?

_____

_____

_____

3. What are the visible signs that reveal Christ and strengthen us in the unity of faith?

_____

_____

_____

4. Describe the beauty, wonder, and joy of being united with our triune God.

_____

_____

_____

5. Why does our heavenly Father call us friend?

_____

_____

_____

---

21 Ephesians 1:11 NLT.

My Journey's Journal:

Part V
Christ's Jubilee

"Consecrate the fiftieth year and proclaim liberty throughout the land to all its inhabitants. It shall be a jubilee for you"
(Leviticus 25:10).

This part of the study guide is dedicated to opening God's story to see Christ of the gospel proclaimed by the Law and prophets. We'll see the Good News that came as the Light, revealed to a people living in the shadow of death so they could see Christ of the Jubilee.

Chapter 21: The Fragrance of the Gospel

Key Scriptures:

- "When she poured this perfume on my body, she did it to prepare me for burial. Truly I tell you, wherever this gospel is preached throughout the world, what she has done will also be told, in memory of her." (Matthew 26:12–13).

- "For we are the aroma of Christ to God among those who are being saved and among those who are perishing, to one a fragrance from death to death, to the other a fragrance from life to life. Who is sufficient for these things?" (2 Corinthians 2:15–16).

Growling stomachs can be heard from every tent in the itinerant camp. When the food truck finally arrives with its aromas of hot coffee, vegetable beef soup, and fresh baked bread, their hungry ribs rejoice. Food aromas are especially potent. They serve as powerful triggers for strongly felt emotions and memories of meals together with family and friends. In the same way, when the fragrance of the gospel flows out, memories of every word, encounter, and testimony of saving grace come to light. Hungry souls breathe in the beautiful fragrance of our Savior.

Christ, who is the Bread of Life, is the central focus of the church. Jesus loved us first and His love compels us to live a lifestyle like Isaiah's fasting.[1] This is more than filling empty stomachs or digging wells for primitive tribes to pump drinking water. We go out to do the work of the Great Commission and raise Christ as our banner. Everything else, from clothing those who shiver in the cold to feeding the hungry and providing medicine for the sick, are outcroppings of the fragrance of Christ's saving grace. They are not the primary mission. We satisfy their natural thirst and then lead them to Christ, the water of life. The aromas of fresh baked bread may wake up their appetite, but the fragrance that draws people to the Bread of Life satisfies hungry souls forever.

> A prayer according to Song of Songs 6:2:
>
> Heavenly Father, help us to know your lovingkindness. Encompass us with the love of the beloved who goes down into the garden to His bride.

---

1 Isaiah 58:7.

We serve the Lord Almighty who is jealous for the renown of His holy name.[2] But He is not concerned for Himself alone. Our heavenly Father gives His name to all who come to saving faith through Jesus Christ. This is our new family name. His zeal for the repute of His name is a family thing. Christ's passion encompasses all who are called by His name. All of God's sons and daughters have a part in exalting God's holy name among the nations and declaring His praises to all people. This is the sweetest fragrance to ever spread its compelling bouquets.

Then, from the farthest corners of the earth, people bring fragrant offerings to present before the God of our salvation. Our witness in word and deeds reveals and reveres God's holy name in every tribe and language.

My name will be great among the nations, from where the sun rises to where it sets. In every place incense and pure offerings will be brought to me, because my name will be great among the nations.
(Malachi 1:11)

Imagine walking through a garden gate where you enjoy the fragrance of cherry blossoms and budding sweet peas. Lilacs drip with sweet bouquets. With every breath, the aromas fill you with delight. Then a gentle breeze comes to spread the sweet aromas to your neighbor.

We are the fragrance of Christ. Christians are like well-watered gardens that abound with the fruit of the Vine, Christ Jesus. The Holy Spirit is the wind that carries the perfumed scents to all those whose lives we touch. The aromas of Christ draw wandering souls to come into God's bountiful garden and partake of its good fruit.

Awake, north wind! Rise up, south wind! Blow on my garden and spread its fragrance all around. Come into your garden, my love; taste its finest fruits.
(Song of Songs 4:16)

We are called to declare Christ's vicarious death until He comes again.[3] The woman who came with "an alabaster jar of expensive perfume,"[4] poured it on Jesus' head while he reclined at the table. The fragrance not only filled that house but every house "wherever this gospel is preached throughout the world,"[5] She anointed her Savior to prepare Him for burial—a death that defeated sin, Satan, and all death. Now we are sent out with the fragrance of Christ to proclaim Jesus' atoning death that offers forgiveness and life to those dead in their transgressions and sin.[6]

Then he opened their minds so they could understand the Scriptures. He told them, "This is what is written: The Messiah will suffer and rise from the dead on

2 Exodus 34:14.
3 1 Corinthians 11:26.
4 Matthew 26:7.
5 Matthew 26:13.
6 Ephesians 2:1.

the third day, and repentance for the forgiveness of sins will be preached in his name to all nations, beginning at Jerusalem. You are witnesses of these things.
(Luke 24:45–48)

We are captives of Christ, discipled to serve as emissaries of His saving grace. By the work of the cross, Jesus redeemed us from captivity to sin and leads us home in a victorious parade. He cleans us up by washing us in His redemptive blood.

Now cleansed, we can spread His sweet fragrance that reveals our Savior everywhere we go. We go to our neighbors so they may see Christ. The church disciples, anoints, and then sends us as witnesses of Jesus' saving grace. Our mission is urgent, because apart from a revelation of Jesus Christ, people perish.[7]

When we proclaim the gospel to the rebellious, we're like a dreadful smell of death.[8] But when we declare Christ crucified to people who are called and chosen, the wind of the Spirit breathes the fragrance of Christ into them. Those who hunger and thirst for the righteousness of Christ welcome and embrace us.

But thanks be to God, who always leads us as captives in Christ's triumphal procession and uses us to spread the aroma of the knowledge of him everywhere. For we are to God the pleasing aroma of Christ among those who are being saved and those who are perishing.
(2 Corinthians 2:14–15)

The powerful effect of the fragrance of Christ spreads out into eternity. It's like a medicine that really does heal and causes many awesome side effects. It brings healing to the brokenhearted.[9] The blind receive sight, the lame walk, the sick are healed, the deaf hear, the dead are raised, and Good News is proclaimed to the poor.[10]

A sure and lasting premise of the Christian church throughout the centuries is our service to the poor. This servant attitude compels us to live an Isaiah kind of fast that denies ourselves so that Christ may be revealed.[11] Jesus said the poor would always be with us.[12] The truth is that if we don't serve the poor, sick, and weak we become proud and forget that we are called to serve.

But with the heart of Christ, we have the attitude of a servant. Our love of Christ compels us to wholeheartedly serve the poor and bring them to the fragrance of Christ.

"All they asked was that we should continue to remember the poor, the very thing I had been eager to do all along."
(Galatians 2:10)

7 Proverbs 29:18.
8 2 Corinthians 2:16 NLT.
9 Psalm 147:3.
10 Matthew 11:5.
11 Isaiah 58:8—9.
12 Mark 14:7.

Christian love flows out with the aromas of Christ. With every breath we breathe, we give wind to balms of saving grace. We give off this aroma every day of our lives. We must not forget the poor and weak among us because this indifference causes fervent faith to crumble into self-serving apathy. If we don't serve the poor, we go blind toward those outside our gilded little circle of friends. The truth is that we need the poor and weak among us to keep our hearts Christlike. Ministering and serving the needs of others strengthens us to endure and minister faithfully.

Our great desire is that you will keep on loving others as long as life lasts, in order to make certain that what you hope for will come true. Then you will not become spiritually dull and indifferent. Instead, you will follow the example of those who are going to inherit God's promises because of their faith and endurance. (Hebrews 6:11–12 NLT)

Jesus' sandals left footprints on the dusty roads of Galilee. His teaching opened people's eyes to see the light in every village, shoreline, and mountainside. People bound in darkness witnessed the Light of the World drive back the shadow of death.[13]

But what lurked in the shadows that encompassed the land? The light of Christ drew the scattered sheep of God's pasture. The indebted, distressed, and discontented came out of the dark into the light of Christ's Jubilee. The sick, lame, and oppressed sought their healer. Our Lord and Savior brought light to drive back the hopeless gloom that permeated the land.

Now, those who are called out of the darkness walk in Jesus' footsteps. The fragrance of Christ radiates out as we proclaim the gospel of Jesus Christ. This delightful aroma compels us to step out as God's sons and daughters to raise a banner and draw people to our Redeemer. His banner draws the poor, weak, and infirm, fully satisfying them. Malcontents, the spiritually impoverished, and those burdened by the weight of sin rally to His banner to be set free. The lawless are called to "obedience that comes from faith."[14]

Follow God's example, therefore, as dearly loved children and walk in the way of love, just as Christ loved us and gave himself up for us as a fragrant offering and sacrifice to God. (Ephesians 5:1–2)

God's holy presence encompasses the ambassadors of God's kingdom as they spread the sweet aromas of Christ. The wind of the Holy Spirit gives us a voice to proclaim the gospel that changes people's daily lives and their eternal destiny. The power of the Word and the Spirit of Christ strengthens us to press on in the work of the Great Commission. The prayers of the saints strengthen our feeble

13 Matthew 4:16.
14 Romans 1:5.

hands and steady our knees[15] so we may raise Christ's banner before the nations to draw all people to Him.[16]

They come spiritually hungry and with empty stomachs. The aromas of fresh bread may draw them to where they receive the sweet fragrance of the Bread of Life. They will taste and see that the Lord is good. People come with growling stomachs, and body and soul are fully satisfied in Christ. They come in limping and go out leaping with joy.

Then I saw another angel flying in midair, and he had the eternal gospel to proclaim to those who live on the earth—to every nation, tribe, language and people. (Revelation 14:6)

When we walk by a restaurant that flows out with scents of smoked barbecue ribs and grilled corn on the cob, the special aromas draw us in. We breathe deep and savor the memories of hometown cooking. Our lives are filled with fragrances that trigger memories of home and hearth. But too often the hope of little children who once knew God's presence have it stolen away by those who hindered them from coming to Jesus.[17] Yet the gospel's compelling sweet perfumes they encounter bring them back home.

Those who are the church ought to live a lifestyle of fasting. They must deny themselves so they can emit the fragrance of Christ. We send these sweet scents along with people who spread the aromas of our Savior to neighbors and nations. Those who are sent to proclaim Christ, the Bread of Life, bring a message that is more satisfying than fresh baked bread to hungry stomachs.

The love of Christ compels us to deny self to keep us from becoming "arrogant, overfed and unconcerned" for the poor.[18] A life of rejecting carnal pleasures and helping others deters us from repeating the sins of Sodom. We provide for those who have material needs, lead them to Christ, and proclaim His redemptive death until He comes again. Providing for the poor and helping the oppressed is like a sweet fragrance—a lifestyle of fasting the Lord has chosen for us.

> This is for a burnt offering, a pleasing aroma, a food offering presented to the Lord.
> (Numbers 28:13)

---

15 Isaiah 35:3.
16 John 12:32.
17 Matthew 19:14.
18 Ezekiel 16:49—50.

Chapter 21 Q&A

The Fragrance of the Gospel

1. How is the sweet fragrance of the gospel spread to every place the sun rises and sets?

_____

_____

_____

2. We emanate the fragrance of Christ, but it is received in different ways. What makes the difference?

_____

_____

_____

3. What is the one premise of the church that has always been and always will be part of our mission?

_____

_____

_____

4. What effect does neglecting the poor have on the church and society?

_____

_____

_____

My Journey's Journal:

Chapter 22: Gospel-Inspired Praise

Key Scriptures:

- "To him who loves us and has freed us from our sins by his blood, and has made us to be a kingdom and priests to serve his God and Father—to him be glory and power for ever and ever! Amen" (Revelation 1:5–6).

- "King of the nations. Who will not fear you, Lord, and bring glory to your name? For you alone are holy. All nations will come and worship before you, for your righteous acts have been revealed" (Revelation 15:3–4).

Triathletes have an obstacle course laid out before them. To compete and win the trophy at the finish line, they build a team of people who excel in various athletic disciplines. But there is one race that receives little acclaim here on earth: the "race marked out for us" by the cross of Jesus Christ.

God strengthens us to press on through every obstacle along the course set before us. Victorious songs of praise strengthen us each step along the way. This part of our Bible excursion opens our eyes to see Christ through the words of David the psalmist and John the revelator. They serve to reveal our Redeemer, the only Son of God, "the champion who initiates and perfects our faith."[1]

Christians rise as a mighty army and rally to our Savior's banner. We're empowered to serve with Him as He drives back the forces of darkness. We are called to march out in the power and strength of the Spirit, shielded with God's armor and singing His praises to the nations.

A prayer according to Zechariah 2:10:

Yahweh our God, may the wind of the Holy Spirit give us voices to sing and be glad, for we are daughters of Zion who await Christ's coming.

Gospel shoes are made to last. The shoestrings won't break when you're getting ready to step out in faith. Shards of rock in the valley of the shadow of death will not penetrate these shoes. We step over mountain-sized obstacles. We will not be discouraged from our mission.

We press on because the Lord God is an ever-present help. He strengthens us in the work of spreading the gospel. The Word lights our pathway, and the Holy Spirit keeps our feet from slipping. With our eyes on the goal, we keep putting

1 Hebrews 12:1—2 NLT.

one foot in front of the other until we reach the summit and raise Christ's banner. Songs of victorious praise go before us, echoing throughout the land. This banner must not be raised in silence, or the rocks will cry out.[2]

We look forward to the New Jerusalem. Its foundations resound with the praise of heaven's choirs. Jasper, sapphire, agate, and emerald adorn the city's foundation, and they echo with the songs of victory. Let us sing out with joy and gladness to exalt the Lord our God. May our hearts leap for joy us as we press on.[3] Every step is graced with praise, taking us "from strength to strength, till each appears before God in Zion."[4]

> *The fear of the Lord is the beginning of wisdom; all who follow his precepts have good understanding. To him belongs eternal praise.*
> (Psalm 111:10).

Jesus came to walk among the people of Israel and announce Good News to the poor and set the oppressed free.[5] He taught and trained His disciples and then sent them out to proclaim God's kingdom. He gave them authority to drive out demons and heal the sick.[6]

Even today, Jesus sends out disciples under His authority to share this healing, restoring, freedom-giving, and life-giving message of salvation. Jesus' command to go, baptize, and make disciples empowers us to do the same work as the twelve and seventy-two disciples who were sent.

The cross we raise as a banner proves to be Christ's true and eternal gospel. This Good News leads to many acts of mercy among an oppressed people. Jesus came as one man, and now He has a countless number of workers whom He sends to neighbors and nations. Their acts of mercy are accomplished by the power and authority of His name and serve to verify the message as true and eternal. Every step we take with our gospel shoes inspires praise, glory, and honor for God's holy name among all who will hear and believe.

> *Very truly I tell you, whoever believes in me will do the works I have been doing, and they will do even greater things than these, because I am going to the Father. And I will do whatever you ask in my name, so that the Father may be glorified in the Son.*
> (John 12:14–15).

We, the church, are sent out to proclaim the greatest message ever heard. Those who are discipled in the church carry the message to their neighbor and to those nearby. Then God's sons and daughters keep going until the Good News is heard to the ends of the earth.[7] Those who follow in Jesus' footsteps sing joy-

---

2 Luke 19:40.
3 Psalm 28:7, 81:1, 118:14.
4 Psalm 84:5—7.
5 Luke 4:18.
6 Luke 9:1—3.
7 Acts 1:8.

fully while suffering on behalf of the cross. We can sing God's praises even when doors get slammed in our faces.

As we suffer with Christ, our troubles prove that we share in His eternal glory. Sorrows inflicted upon us confirm that we have an inheritance in the kingdom of heaven. With this great hope, we hold onto God's promises and sing out in harmony with God's eternal glory. With psalms of salvation on our lips, we lead many to righteousness so they may shine out like the stars for ever and ever.[8]

Now if we are children, then we are heirs—heirs of God and co-heirs with Christ, if indeed we share in his sufferings in order that we may also share in his glory. (Romans 8:17).

By grace and through faith we come to the fountain that flows with living water to make us new creations in Christ. Long ago, the Word spoke and created all things. By this same Word we are born from above. In the waters of baptism and by the power of the Word, we die to our self, we are buried with Christ, and then raised up in resurrection power. We are made one with the Father, Son, and Holy Spirit who indwells us. We're adopted into the family of God, and He gives us His name. A white stone is given to the victorious as assurance and proof that they are absolved of all guilt.[9] The Holy Spirit's seal is a great and precious promise given to us in writing.[10]

Our hearts overflow with praise even before our eyes open to the morning light. We shout out songs of exaltation with the rising of the sun. A holy people lift holy hands with songs when the sun is high above. Children of resurrection sing with thanksgiving as the family comes together to join the amity around the dinner table. People of faith honor our heavenly Father with glorious refrains as the sun slips below the horizon. Then all the redeemed sing out with words of eternal faith and hope as we gather with the sons and daughters of promise in the congregation.

He saved us through the washing of rebirth and renewal by the Holy Spirit, whom he poured out on us generously through Jesus Christ our Savior, so that, having been justified by his grace, we might become heirs having the hope of eternal life. (Titus 3:5–7)

We build on a sure foundation, that is Christ Jesus, our eternal and unshakeable rock. The storms of life pound against us. Waves of the world's chaos crash around us like ocean breakers against weather-worn rocks. But there is a lighthouse built into the bedrock on the shoreline that withstands the most perilous storms.

Life's troubles cannot shake our faith because the Rock, who is our hope, is a firm and secure anchor for our soul.[11] We fix our eyes on Christ, the rejected

8 Daniel 12:3.
9 Revelation 2:17.
10 Ephesians 1:13.
11 Hebrews 6:19.

stone who is now the Cornerstone.[12] He is the precious Cornerstone upon whom we can build a new and abundant life filled with songs of praise that drive back the world's chaos. =

As you come to him, the living Stone–rejected by humans but chosen by God and precious to him–you also, like living stones, are being built into a spiritual house to be a holy priesthood, offering spiritual sacrifices acceptable to God through Jesus Christ. For in Scripture it says: "See, I lay a stone in Zion, a chosen and precious corner-stone, and the one who trusts in him will never be put to shame."
(1 Peter 2:4–6).

"The night is nearly over; the day is almost here."[13] The troops are willing and ready on the day of battle, and they march out with praises, arrayed in holy splendor.[14] Soldiers of the cross appear like dew from the womb of the morning. The Lord, who is mighty in battle, is at our right hand, and He crushes every stronghold that opposes His kingdom of righteousness.[15]

The severity of God's judgment against His enemies offends our natural sensibilities. But then, when we see the enemy shooting his fiery darts with deadly intent against God's people, we know that we serve a God of justice. The Almighty's army rises to their feet to call people out of the darkness with an earth-shaking shout, "Rise up, Lord! May your enemies be scattered."[16]

In the strength of the Spirit, we remain true to the gospel of Christ and the cross to the very end. By the power of the Word and the Holy Spirit we stand strong, submitted to serve under the authority of Christ victorious.

To the one who is victorious and does my will to the end, I will give authority over the nations–that one "will rule them with an iron scepter and will dash them to pieces like pottery"–just as I have received authority from my Father. I will also give that one the morning star.
(Revelation 2:26–28)

We raise Christ's banner above this dry and thirsty land. Our feet struggle through crusted desert terrain. Parched ground breaks under our feet. Every step stirs up dust to blur our vision. But the Great I AM raises a mighty army to press on as we see the day approaching.[17] We long for our heavenly Father and earnestly seek Him who satisfies us in this dry and thirsty land.[18] We thirst for living water so that we may never thirst again.

---

12 Psalm 118:22.
13 Romans 13:12.
14 Psalm 110:3.
15 Psalm 110:5.
16 Numbers 10:35.
17 Hebrews 10:25.
18 Isaiah 44:3.

We come to the source, the One who provides an oasis: a place of rest. In this resting place, we see that His love is better than life. From the wellsprings of our heart and soul we sing out to glorify our Lord and Savior. In this place of safety, the richest of foods satisfies us, and we sing out with eternal praise.[19]

Now our Good Shepherd leads His lambs beside still water. The sheep of His pasture drink from still waters and then sound out their praises. Indeed, we are victors in Christ, so we may look forward to that awesome day when He will sing out with a victorious song, "It is done."

He said to me: "It is done. I am the Alpha and the Omega, the Beginning and the End. To the thirsty I will give water without cost from the spring of the water of life. Those who are victorious will inherit all this, and I will be their God and they will be my children. (Revelation 21:6–7).

Fasten gospel shoes on your feet to prepare for the race marked out for you.[20] God's sons and daughters see the way forward to their inheritance with eyes of faith. We step out with songs of praise overflowing from our hearts. Children of resurrection join the procession along the way of praise as they ascend to the mountain of the Lord to raise His banner.

Jesus commissioned us to go and make disciples, and by His command we have the authority to press on and proclaim Christ's Jubilee. We take up His gospel message and then see it proven true with signs, wonders, and spiritual gifts for the church.

We lift our hands from the dust and grime of this dry and thirsty land, and Christ's cleansing fount refreshes us. God's people have a Rock upon whom we stand, a place of safety where we anchor our souls. We hold fast to Christ, the beginning and end of all things. He is the Good Shepherd who leads us in paths of righteousness until the great day when we receive our eternal inheritance.

With every sunrise until sunset and through the night we sing out with loud voices accompanied by the angels in heaven: "the kingdom of the world has become the kingdom of our Lord and of his Messiah, and He will reign for ever and ever."[21]

Sing to the Lord a new song, for he has done marvelous things; his right hand and his holy arm have worked salvation for him. The Lord has made his salvation known and revealed his righteousness to the nations. (Psalm 98:1–2)

19 Psalm 63:3—5.
20 Hebrews 12:1.
21 Revelation 11:15.

Chapter 22 Q&A

Gospel-Inspired Praise

1. How do we go from strength to strength as we do the impossible work of the Great Commission?

_____

_____

_____

2. Describe the special qualities of the gospel shoes provided for your feet.

_____

_____

_____

3. How does suffering for the cause of Christ and the cross serve God's good purpose?

_____

_____

_____

4. When you hear the sweet words of the gospel's message of hope, what songs of praise overflow from your heart?

_____

_____

_____

My Journey's Journal:

Chapter 23: The Year of the Lord's Favor

Key Scriptures:

- "The Spirit of the Sovereign Lord is on me, because the Lord has anointed me to proclaim good news to the poor. He has sent me to bind up the brokenhearted, to proclaim freedom for the captives and release from darkness for the prisoners, to proclaim the year of the Lord's favor and the day of vengeance of our God, to comfort all who mourn, and provide for those who grieve in Zion—to bestow on them a crown of beauty instead of ashes, the oil of joy instead of mourning, and a garment of praise instead of a spirit of despair. They will be called oaks of righteousness, a planting of the Lord for the display of his splendor" (Isaiah 61:1–3).

- "'The Spirit of the LORD is on me, because he has anointed me to proclaim good news to the poor. He has sent me to proclaim freedom for the prisoners and recovery of sight for the blind, to set the oppressed free, to proclaim the year of the LORD's favor.' Then he rolled up the scroll, gave it back to the attendant and sat down. The eyes of everyone in the synagogue were fastened on him. He began by saying to them, 'Today this scripture is fulfilled in your hearing'" (Luke 4:18–21).

A lot of kids grew up with Mom's dinner time rule: If we didn't answer her call to come to the table when she served the food, we missed out on a good, hot meal. Surely Mom got this wisdom right out of her Bible. She learned from the Creator, who set the heavens and earth in order when time began.

The Word of creation established a time of favor for each one of us. The psalmist teaches us to rightly consider the number of our days to gain wisdom, that is Christ who is our Jubilee. Each one of us is given a time that is right, a day of favor. The moment when our ears open to hear the Good News of saving grace is our "today." We must not put off the gospel's call until tomorrow, because neither striving, worry nor procrastination will add a single day to our life.[1]

When our ears are opened to hear the gospel, Christ is revealed. This is our moment of the Lord's favor. It's the hour of salvation. Don't put it off. We don't know what tomorrow holds for us. On this day, the Word and the Holy Spirit lead us into grace, redemption, and our time of deliverance.

---

1 Matthew 6:27.

Israel's year of Jubilee foreshadowed this great season of the Lord's favor when they proclaimed liberty for those in bondage. In the fiftieth-year people were set free to return to their ancestral lands.

A prayer according to Psalm 90:17:

Oh, Lord our God, may your favor rest upon us to establish the work of our hands. Yes, oh, Lord, establish the good work of our hands you have begun in us.

If we understood how readily our heavenly Father forgives us, we would not be so reluctant to acknowledge and confess our sins. We tend to get all stirred up and guilt ridden because of our failings. Do we get something out of carrying our faults around with us like a backpack full of rocks? Why do we wait so long to surrender and come back to find rest where there is sweet fellowship with our Lord and God?

In confession and repentance, we break through to the heavens that were once like brass when we prayed.[2] The joy of being pardoned brings us into unity that's like a pleasant oil poured over our head and running down into the beard.[3] When our sin is absolved, it's like the sunrise that drives back the darkness.

Forgiven and cleansed people are like those lifted out of turbulent, raging flood water and then led beside still waters. Don't wait and miss out on God's abundant grace. Today is the day to confess our sin and enter the joy of His salvation.

Then I acknowledged my sin to you and did not cover up my iniquity. I said, "I will confess my transgressions to the Lord." And you forgave the guilt of my sin. Therefore let all the faithful pray to you while you may be found; surely the rising of the mighty waters will not reach them.
(Psalm 32:5–6)

Our friends at the pub may sing their heckling songs and laugh at the mention of our name after we stop joining them in their late-night revelries. But our resolve remains solid. We gave up indulgent partying to remain in Christ who is Lord of our lives.

The Word and the Spirit reveal Christ to us, and by faith we enter God's eternal favor. In our distress and misery, we see our need of a Savior. In the day of our salvation, He hears our cry for help and brings us into His bountiful love.

But I pray to you, Lord, in the time of your favor; in your great love, O God, answer me with your sure salvation.
(Psalm 69:13)

We must take care and not miss the moment we're called into sweet communion with the Father, Son, and Holy Spirit. This is the season for us to gather

---

2 Deuteronomy 28:23.
3 Psalm 133:1—2.
162

with the congregation to worship in God's house of prayer and confess our sins one to the other so that we may be healed. This is the time for admitting our offenses so we may be forgiven. Gathering to worship brings us into Christ's holy presence for a time of worship and prayer in agreement with each other and God's Word. This unity refreshes His love in us and brings us into times of sweet communion with Jesus our High Priest, who is actively present to minister before us and hear our petitions.

> *Let the peace of Christ be in control in your heart (for you were in fact called as one body to this peace), and be thankful. Let the word of Christ dwell in you richly, teaching and exhorting one another with all wisdom, singing psalms, hymns, and spiritual songs, all with grace in your hearts to God.*
> (Colossians 3:15—16)

We've made a big mess of things by dishonoring Christ as Lord of our lives. Our selfish ways have separated us from fellowship with our Father.[4] Instead of seeking God's righteousness for the sake of His name, we seek our own pleasure above all else.[5] We no longer walk in the fear of the Lord. Our feet slipped from Jesus' narrow pathway, and our prayers are not heard.[6]

We're seriously in need of repentance, forgiveness, cleansing, and restoration. Don't wait. Never hesitate. Stop putting it off. Today is your day to recognize, admit, and confess your sin and receive forgiveness.

We must not be like the people of God's holy nation. Isaiah spoke Yahweh's oracles to them, "In repentance and rest is your salvation, in quietness and trust is your strength." But they "would have none of it."[7] They rejected the blessings of God's Jubilee.

> *This is what the Lord says: "In the time of my favor I will answer you, and in the day of salvation I will help you; I will keep you and will make you to be a covenant for the people, to restore the land and to reassign its desolate inheritances."*
> (Isaiah 49:8)

There is no day better than today to enter our Father's eternal kingdom. He brings us into a realm that abounds in grace, mercy, healing, and restoration. We've wandered away from the flock and got ourselves caught in life's glitter and glam that turns into thorns and thistles. Today is the day of your salvation. This is the moment when the voice of the Good Shepherd's saving grace beckons you. Eternity calls out to you today.

God's faithful messengers preach the Good News so you may hear. The seed of faith is planted in your heart. Will you believe and not deny the truth? Now is

---

4 Isaiah 59:2.
5 James 4:3.
6 John 9:31.
7 Isaiah 30:15.

your time to enter the joy of the Lord's saving grace. Today, while it is called today is your day—your season of grace. Tomorrow doesn't belong to you. We don't know what happens tomorrow. So, "Come all who are thirsty, come to the waters."[8]

As God's co-workers we urge you not to receive God's grace in vain. For he says, "In the time of my favor I heard you, and in the day of salvation I helped you." I tell you, now is the time of God's favor, now is the day of salvation.
(2 Corinthians 6:1–2)

The apostle Paul wrote the following verses to Titus. They're packed with truths that begin at creation and reach out into eternity. They are as timeless as they are timely. They lead us to our eternal hope and speak to us in the moment of God's favor.

As the Word spoke the first words of creation, the Creator recorded the names of all those He would adopt as sons and daughters throughout all time. The Great I AM created all the heavens and earth and on the seventh day rested from His work.

When He sat down to rest, He made a place for us to enter His rest. In the first words of creation, our heavenly Father prepared a way of redemption through His only Son—the perfect and acceptable sacrifice for the sins of a fallen world. Look back to creation and then out into eternity with eyes of hope opened by the power of God's Word so we may "encourage one another daily, as long as it is called 'Today.'"[9]

Paul, a servant of God and an apostle of Jesus Christ to further the faith of God's elect and their knowledge of the truth that leads to godliness–in the hope of eternal life, which God, who does not lie, promised before the beginning of time, and which now at his appointed season he has brought to light through the preaching entrusted to me by the command of God our Savior.
(Titus 1:1–3)

When you commute from New York City to Long Island, if you don't follow the train schedules and get on right trains, you'll get lost in the crowds. God's kingdom doesn't depend on man's schedules to get you to your eternal destination, but He sets the days before you and prepares a way that leads you to your day of redemption. You don't know the season or the hour when Jesus will return.[10] You don't know when you'll take your last breath. So you need to be dressed, ready, and waiting.[11] The Scriptures instruct Christians to be ready today so you don't miss the great gathering that takes you to our eternal home.[12]

For, "In just a little while, he who is coming will come and will not delay."
(Hebrews 10:37)

8 Isaiah 55:1.
9 Hebrews 3:13.
10 Matthew 24:36, 1 Thessalonians 5:1.
11 Luke 12:35—40.
12 Mark 13:27.

If you want to get from Anacortes, Washington, to Victoria, BC, you have to arrive at the dock on time to get your car on the ferry. The time of departure is set in advance, and the captain will not wait for those who linger. If you miss the boat, you'll also miss the playful orca whales in the Puget Sound and the beauty of Butchart Gardens.

The apostle Paul's inspired letters still offer guiding light to Christians today. The inspired words of Scripture he penned on parchment contain truths established in the beginning and remain true even when Christ returns for His own. He makes it clear that the Creator recorded our names in heaven's book and appointed a time for us to hear the gospel's call and be born again of the Spirit. We are new creations, adopted, given a new name and united with Christ in His church so we may encourage God's sons and daughters in the faith in a moment of opportunity.

> But encourage one another daily, as long as it is called 'Today,' so that none of you may be hardened by sin's deceitfulness. (Hebrews 3:13)

Chapter 23 Q&A

The Year of the Lord's Favor

1. Describe the joy of being forgiven and cleansed?

_____

_____

_____

2. Does Christ's Jubilee apply even today?

_____

_____

_____

3. How do you know when it's your "Today" and Christ is calling you to saving grace?

_____

_____

_____

4. When was your name written in heaven's Book of Life?

_____

_____

_____

My Journey's Journal:

Chapter 24: Our Kinsman-Redeemer

Key Scriptures:

- "If one of your fellow Israelites becomes poor and sells some of their property, their nearest relative is to come and redeem what they have sold" (Leviticus 25:25).

- "The Word became flesh and made his dwelling among us. We have seen his glory, the glory of the one and only Son, who came from the Father, full of grace and truth" (John 1:4).

There is a special bond that is only possible when you're family. When kids play with brothers, sisters, and cousins, there's a sense of relationship that rarely happens even with best friends. Kids with their kin share a special kind of crazy. Then when they grow up, there is a connection that compels them to reach out and help each other when they see their family in trouble or in need.

God provided a kinsman-redeemer—our elder brother, Jesus Christ, the only Son of God.[1] How did He come to be kin with us? He gave up His glory in heaven and came down to share in our humanity.[2] How did He become Redeemer? He gave His body to be broken and His life blood to be shed to pay the price for our sin debt. He took upon Himself our penalty; the wages of our deadly sin.[3] He walked among us with love and compassion and then gave Himself as the perfect Lamb of God, the Passover lamb, to redeem us from bondage to sin, Satan, and death. He could only do this for us as a kinsman-redeemer.

> A prayer according to Philippians 2:9:
>
> God of our salvation, by the power of the Word and the Holy Spirit, open our eyes, ears, and understanding so we may have faith to believe our Lord Jesus, who is exalted above all and whose name is above every name.

The Word of creation, the only Son of God, "did not consider equality with God something to be grasped." He took on a human nature with flesh, blood, and bone. He looked like us and talked the language. Jesus humbled Himself, leaving heaven behind to become a man. Now, all those who will believe and receive Him by faith, as Lord and Savior, are His kin. He is our elder brother,

---

1 Mark 3:34.
2 Hebrews 2:14—15.
3 Romans 6:23.

our nearest relative, our kinsman-redeemer. He saves us from the deadly sin that enslaved us and restores all that once belonged to us.[4]

Every kinsman-redeemer foreshadowed Christ who came to redeem us. Jesus fulfilled the Levitical law that restored their brother's inheritance by making us heirs according to the promise.[5]

The land must not be sold permanently, because the land is mine and you reside in my land as foreigners and strangers. Throughout the land that you hold as a possession, you must provide for the redemption of the land. If one of your fellow Israelites becomes poor and sells some of their property, their nearest relative is to come and redeem what they have sold.
(Leviticus 25:23–25)

Job suffered enormous losses and then endured volumes of insults to his integrity from so-called friends. His own wife urged him to curse God and die rather than suffer.[6] But Job knew that the ground he stood on belonged to the Lord. He rose and stood his ground to proclaim kinship with his living Redeemer. He remained firm in his faith and called out to the One who could restore all that was lost and stolen.

His friends were wrong about him. His wife wounded him with her counsel. But Job's eyes stayed focused on the One who saves and restores. Thousands of years before Christ was born among mankind, Job spoke some of the most powerful words of faith recorded in the holy Scriptures.

I know that my redeemer lives, and that in the end he will stand on the earth.
(Job 19:25)

Family farmers all around the world have a deep sense of connection to the land. Their roots are deep in the fields they plow, harrow, seed, water, and then harvest. They conserve and protect the boundaries they inherited from their fathers because this is their roots and livelihood. Their children grow up with their feet planted on this plot of soil that connects them to the past, provides for them in the present, and then gets passed on to the next generation.

God created Adam from the dust of the ground.[7] Yahweh called Abram to go to a land he didn't know. Moses led the tribes of Israel to a Promised Land that flowed with milk and honey. Isaiah prophesied of a land, saying, "No longer will they call you Deserted, or name your land Desolate. But you will be called Hephzibah, and your land Beulah;[8] for the Lord will take delight in you, and your land will be married.[9]

4 Philippians 2:6—8.
5 Galatians 3:29.
6 Job 2:9.
7 Genesis 2:7.
8 Hephzibah means, "My delight is in her." Beulah means, "Married, or married to the land."
9 Isaiah 62:4.

But sin stole away our inheritance and enslaved us, as if captured in a foreign land. We were far away and in serious need of a Redeemer. But praise be to God, for He made a way through the sea. He calls us by name and holds back the flood waters of the river. He brings us safely through the fire into His land of promise He has redeemed on our behalf.[10]

> But now, this is what the Lord says–he who created you, Jacob, he who formed you, Israel: "Do not fear, for I have redeemed you; I have summoned you by name; you are mine."
>
> (Isaiah 43:1)

Come, gather at the gates of the city where we celebrate with a victorious parade. Join the throng of celebrants who wave palm branches as they dance and sing in the streets. Christ Jesus extends his hands to every tribe and nation to bring them home in a triumphant procession. They bring His sons in their arms and carry His daughters on their shoulders, restoring them to the land of promise.

Our Savior came in the flesh to serve as our very own kinsman-redeemer. The oppression of sin stole us away, but now Christ victorious ascends on high, brings us home in joyful celebration as captives in His train, and gives us good gifts from the plunder.[11]

> Thus says the Lord God: "Behold, I will lift up my hand to the nations, and raise my signal to the peoples; and they shall bring your sons in their arms, and your daughters shall be carried on their shoulders.
> (Isaiah 49:22 ESV)

Jesus was born of the Spirit by virgin Mary, fully human and fully God. He lived and ministered among us and opened blind eyes to see "His glory, the glory of the one and only Son, who came from the Father, full of grace and truth."[12] He came to serve as our kinsman-redeemer, so that He may redeem us as His own and restore all that once belonged to us.

Jesus could not be our Redeemer if He was not our kin. He could not be our Savior unless His body was lifted up on a cruel Roman cross. The nails and spear that pierced Him caused His life blood to flow, washing away the sins of the world.

> "And I, when I am lifted up from the earth, will draw all people to myself." He said this to show the kind of death he was going to die.
> (John 12:32–33)

The sacrificial blood of the Lamb of God and the waters of baptism make us one with the Father, Son, and Holy Spirit. Now we are temples where the Holy Spirit dwells. Our Lord Jesus, the Word, dwells in us richly,[13] taking up residence

---

10 Isaiah 43:2—3.
11 Psalm 68:18, Ephesians 4:8.
12 John 1:14.
13 Colossians 3:16.

in our earthen tents. Jesus gave His body to be broken and shed His blood to pay the debt of our sin in full. He purchased us out of slavery to sin and restores us. How can we do any less than to honor our Redeemer in all that we do and say?

Do you not know that your bodies are temples of the Holy Spirit, who is in you, whom you have received from God? You are not your own; you were bought at a price. Therefore honor God with your bodies.
(1 Corinthians 6:19–20)

Are you among the redeemed? Has the Father adopted you as a child of promise? Has our Lord and Savior restored good gifts to you? Are you set free from the chains of sin? Is your sin debt paid in full? Indeed, you are abundantly restored in God's land of promise. Through saving faith in Jesus Christ, you are Abraham's seed, a seed of faith that makes you an heir with an eternal promise. Join with the captives in a victorious procession, for Christ is lifted up. He arose victorious over every realm of darkness. Every stronghold, all authorities, powers of this dark world, and spiritual forces of evil have been defeated,[14] and placed under Jesus' feet.[15]

Now all people of saving faith stand together as one in Christ. You are all equal among God's redeemed. Whether you're incarcerated, working in a coal mine deep in the earth, or standing on a stage before the nation; if you have come to saving faith in Jesus Christ, you stand shoulder to shoulder with your Redeemer before your heavenly Father. This is the good work of our kinsman-redeemer.

There is neither Jew nor Gentile, neither slave nor free, nor is there male and female, for you are all one in Christ Jesus. If you belong to Christ, then you are Abraham's seed, and heirs according to the promise.
(Galatians 3:28–29)

Rejoice, and again I say, rejoice. We are restored to our eternal inheritance by Jesus Christ, our kinsman who paid our sin debt to redeem us. Jesus can be our Savior because He came to be our kin, our elder brother. Come, join in our Redeemer's triumphant procession for He has conquered and plundered our enemies. He rescues those who are captives, brings them home in a joyful procession, and gives them good gifts. Those who were once captive to sin and condemned to death are restored to their eternal inheritance in our heavenly Father's land of promise.

> The living, the living—they praise you, as I am doing today; parents tell their children about your faithfulness. (Isaiah 38:19).

---

14 Ephesians 6:12.
15 Ephesians 1:22.

Chapter 24 Q&A

Our Kinsman-Redeemer

1. Could Jesus redeem us if He was not our kin?

_____

_____

_____

2. What is the significance of Christ's victorious procession with captives in His train?

_____

_____

_____

3. What price did our Savior pay to redeem us from sin's debt?

_____

_____

_____

4. Why does Job's powerful declaration of faith continue to ring true as it echoes through the centuries?

_____

_____

_____

My Journey's Journal:

Part VI
Finish the Work

"My food," said Jesus, "is to do the will of him who sent me and to finish his work." (John 4:34)

The work of the Great Commission is not complete, which means that the church is not yet fully established. As we press on in this part of our learning adventure, we'll see the many good things the Spirit of Christ empowers us to do as we confront the unique challenges of the work of God's kingdom in our day.

Chapter 25: Defend the Faith

Key Scriptures:

- "But in your hearts revere Christ as Lord. Always be prepared to give an answer to everyone who asks you to give the reason for the hope that you have. But do this with gentleness and respect" (1 Peter 3:15).

- "Be wise in the way you act toward outsiders; make the most of every opportunity. Let your conversation be always full of grace, seasoned with salt, so that you may know how to answer everyone" (Colossians 4:5–6).

If your new saxophone makes strange sounds, you should learn to read music and then practice. When your count of lost golf balls is as high as your score, you need to practice. A winning basketball team requires a lot of work. Practice, prepare, train, exercise, and repeat. Those who desire to be good at defending our faith in Jesus Christ must learn to draw their strength from the Holy Spirit who teaches, trains, and prepares us before sending us into the fray.

Whether you're learning public speaking or training for competition, you become good at it through exercising your gift and then consistently doing what you learned. The Holy Spirit finds useful ambassadors of Christ among those who are being saturated with God's Word and prepared with words of hope ready to speak. The best messengers are those who are gentle, respectful, gracious, and very salty.

A prayer according to Matthew 15:16:

Father in heaven, may the fire of the Spirit burn in our hearts so we will shine out with the light of Christ before others in all we do and say.

Without revelation, the people run amok and soon perish.[1] Can those blinded to the truth see Christ? Can they hear the message of the gospel if their ears are not opened to hear? The Good News sounds like nonsense to ears stopped up with rebellion. The light of life is shrouded in darkness to spiritually blind eyes. Revelation is only possible by the work of the Holy Spirit who reveals Christ. The Spirit of Jesus opens the way to kingdom treasures and riches stored in secret places so that people may hear the Father calling them by name.[2]

---

1 Proverbs 29:18.
2 Isaiah 45:3.

Those who defend the faith need to be aware of this reality and get prepared. Not everyone will have their eyes opened to the truth. Only a few will hear the message.[3] When people do reject the truth and throw out the messenger, we leave them behind in the dust.[4]

> *The person without the Spirit does not accept the things that come from the Spirit of God but considers them foolishness, and cannot understand them because they are discerned only through the Spirit.*
> (1 Corinthians 2:14

When apostle Paul traveled to a new town, he went to the local synagogue where the faithful gathered. He opened the Scriptures to them so the Holy Spirit could reveal Christ, their Messiah. He preached a Savior who came in the flesh and gave His body to be broken and His blood to be shed. He revealed a Savior as their Passover lamb, the Lamb of God who was slain from the foundations of the world.[5]

But not everyone would hear. Their traditions were too precious, and many turned against him. Paul was stoned, plotted against, accused, and arrested. But even a tormenting thorn in his flesh could not restrain him.[6] A prison's chains could not keep him from proclaiming Christ and defending the faith. He used his chains as an opportunity to give witness of his Lord and Savior. Whether Paul was in a house of prayer or locked in a dungeon, the light of Christ could not be extinguished. He continued to defend his faith in every circumstance.

> *As was his custom, Paul went into the synagogue, and on three Sabbath days he reasoned with them from the Scriptures, explaining and proving that the Messiah had to suffer and rise from the dead. "This Jesus I am proclaiming to you is the Messiah," he said.*
> (Acts 17:2–3)

Moments of discouragement trouble all ambassadors of Christ. It often seems that all their hard work produces nothing but distress. Champions of the cross must hold onto God's promises, knowing that when we proclaim God's Word it is never ineffective or in vain. Gospel messengers encounter those who are "ever hearing, but never understanding, ever seeing, but never perceiving."[7] But we are assured that the power of the gospel will accomplish all that God desires and achieve the purpose for which He sent it.[8]

In the Spirit of Christ we have the means to be constant and resolute while pressing on in the work of the Great Commission. The impossible mission of the

---

3 Matthew 22:14.
4 Luke 9:5.
5 Revelation 13:8.
6 2 Corinthians 12:7.
7 Isaiah 6:9.
8 Isaiah 55:11.

church becomes possible by the dynamos of the Spirit of Christ. The work cannot be accomplished by human strength or mortal power, but by means of the empowering work of the Holy Spirit.

Therefore, my beloved brothers, be steadfast, immovable, always abounding in the work of the Lord, knowing that in the Lord your labor is not in vain.
(1 Corinthians 15:58 ESV)

When people misinterpret parts of the Bible and then spout off with untruths, we don't defend our faith by saying, "That's not what they taught me in Sunday School." It's important for maturing Christians to diligently study God's Word with the mind of Christ and with the Holy Spirit as our teacher. With the Scriptures hidden in our hearts and ready on the tip of our tongues, we're prepared to speak out the truths of the gospel and defend our faith in Jesus Christ. We can stand up for our faith because we are witnesses of God's power and might to save as evidenced in our own lives.

Since, then, we know what it is to fear the Lord, we try to persuade others. What we are is plain to God, and I hope it is also plain to your conscience.
(2 Corinthians 5:11)

Remember that when you defend the faith to spiritually dead people, manmade methods have no effect on them. When upholding the truth and speaking God's Word, it never makes sense until the Holy Spirit gives them ears to hear. The people to whom you witness are dead in their sins and have no means of their own to hear and believe. Spiritually dead people can't understand what you're saying until the Holy Spirit gives wind to the gospel message you speak. The Word and the Spirit reveal Christ, giving life to those are spiritually deaf and blind.

As for you, you were dead in your transgressions and sins.
(Ephesians 2:1)

If a spiritually dead person tries to read the Bible, the words are just print on a page until the Holy Spirit awakens them and plants the seed of faith in their heart. The Spirit of Jesus sends the right person to open the Scriptures for them. The Spirit gives witnesses gospel shoes to step out at the right time and in the right place.

Paul's letter to the Romans asks a very crucial question of those whose feet go out with the message of Christ's power and might to save.

But how can they call on him to save them unless they believe in him? And how can they believe in him if they have never heard about him? And how can they hear about him unless someone tells them? And how will anyone go and tell them without being sent? That is why the Scriptures say, "How beautiful are the feet of messengers who bring good news!"
(Romans 10:14–15)

Your naturally charismatic personality does not persuade people to come to Christ. They don't come to know Jesus as Lord and Savior because you drive a luxury car with a "Jesus Saves" bumper sticker. Lost sheep don't come into the fold because you offer them proofs regarding the Bible's historic evidence. Changing lives for eternity is only possible because the Holy Spirit reveals God's great love toward them and sends someone to testify of a heavenly Father who abounds in saving grace. Lost souls see that something is missing in their lives when they watch those who are alive in Christ walk humbly, forgiven, and cleansed.

> *But because of his great love for us, God, who is rich in mercy, made us alive with Christ even when we were dead in transgressions—it is by grace you have been saved.* (Ephesians 2:4–5)

Christians, properly prepared as disciples, can boldly profess Jesus Christ as Lord and Savior, even in the face of fierce opposition. They are ready to serve as witnesses to their neighbors, to their fellow workers, at the corporate office, and to coworkers at the company's international branches in other nations. They're equipped to serve as a witness at the machine shop where they work, in their neighborhood, and at the company Christmas party. We are sent out to defend the faith to "whoever has ears" so they can hear what the Spirit says to His church.[9] We add nothing to the message, nor do we take anything away from it, speaking truth that we hear the Spirit speaking so we may proclaim Christ vicarious death until He comes again.[10]

> *Dear friends, although I was very eager to write to you about the salvation we share, I felt compelled to write and urge you to contend for the faith that was once for all entrusted to God's holy people.* (Jude 1:3)

Is it possible for a man to bind Pleiades with chains?[11] Can any man or woman contend with the Almighty to correct Him?[12] These rhetorical questions offer proof that the gospel we proclaim to neighbors and nations cannot be chained. No one can lock it away. It's not possible to banish God's Word. Champions of the cross may be arrested or locked in a dungeon, but the Good News message of Christ and the cross will never be snuffed out.

When arrested, the apostle Paul vigorously defended his faith in Jesus Christ before rulers and tribunals. The guards chained to Paul became a perfect audience to hear the gospel's message of saving grace.

---

9 Revelation 2:17.
10 1 Corinthians 11:26.
11 Job 38:31.
12 Job 40:1.

With the same confidence, we press on to proclaim Christ's vicarious death until He comes again. We put on God's armor and unsheathe the sword of the Spirit—the Word of God—and brandish it before the nations. When confronted with fierce opposition, we press on to defend the truth that lives in us. We proclaim God's Word, knowing that sowing the good gospel seeds always accomplishes all that our God has planned with great purpose.

> The Lord Almighty has sworn, "Surely, as I have planned, so it will be, and as I have purposed, so it will happen." (Isaiah 14:24)

Chapter 25 Q&A

Defend the Faith

1. Why does the gospel message sound like nonsense to some people?

_____

_____

_____

2. What methods should we avoid when defending our faith?

_____

_____

_____

3. Try to imagine what it was like to be a Roman guard chained to the apostle Paul.

_____

_____

_____

4. What must we do to prepare ourselves to defend the faith?

_____

_____

_____

My Journey's Journal:

Chapter 26: Declare His Mighty Works

Key Scriptures:

- "So do not be ashamed of the testimony about our Lord or of me his prisoner. Rather, join with me in suffering for the gospel, by the power of God" (2 Timothy 1:8).

- "Arise, shine, for your light has come, and the glory of the Lord rises upon you. See, darkness covers the earth and thick darkness is over the peoples, but the Lord rises upon you and his glory appears over you. Nations will come to your light, and kings to the brightness of your dawn" Isaiah 60:1–3).

Declaring the saving work of our Lord and Savior is a daunting challenge because of all the daily demands on our time and attention. Cell phone notifications chime constantly. We come home from work, drive into the garage, and close the garage door to shut out the world's noise. Then, after dinner we move to the media room, check out our social media contacts, click "like" on our friend's "I love Jesus" post, and then tune out and doze off while trying to watch a ball game.

Reaching the lost through social media while sitting on our couch is ineffective. Email blasts just add to our friend's information overload. Social media is great to keep in touch with family but is too impersonal when it comes to changing a person's eternal destiny. The chances are little better than none that our followers on social media will enter through our church doors. What they really need is a personal connection, a relationship, and that's increasingly difficult in an online world.

We are called to shine out to display the light and glory of Christ. Proclaiming God's mighty works drives back the creeping darkness that invades our nation. Speaking words of grace and mercy heals the wounds of God's people and heals the land of people's pervasive curses.[1] We are called to leave everything else behind and suffer for the gospel's sake so that all may hear of God's mighty works, His power to save, and the glory of God's holy name.

---

1 Isaiah 24:5—6.

A prayer according to Ephesians 6:20:

Father of light, armor up your sons and daughters so we may boldly declare your mighty work of saving grace to this generation.

When we resonate with songs of praise from our spirit and in accord with all truth, the Holy Spirit stirs the hearts of those who hear of His mighty works. Church musicians playing in harmony with the Spirit of Christ and in accord with His promises lift the hearts of God's people. Worshipful exaltations from the congregation unite the hearts of all those who are joined together in a common faith. Our exaltations flow out with awesome words of "Amazing grace, how sweet the sound."[2]

It is good to praise the Lord and make music to your name, O Most High. (Psalm 92:1)

Wherever we lay our heads at night, at home or away, God's Word is the theme of our song.[3] In the morning we throw open the windows and sing out with choruses of our heavenly Father's amazing love. Then, after the sun sets, we rap out with lyrical proclamations of the Lord s faithfulness and the awesome work of His mighty hand and outstretched arm.

Proclaiming your love in the morning and your faithfulness at night. (Psalm 92:2)

Whether our praises are accompanied by a lyre, harp, acoustic guitars, or a grand piano, the congregation offers songs of God's faithfulness, love, and saving grace with melodious harmonies. God's people gather on a day of rest where they join their voices with musical instruments to celebrate the Great I AM. We celebrate the Word of creation, who spoke all things into being.[4] We exalt the Alpha and Omega, who is the beginning of all good things and our everlasting rest.

We don't sing for ourselves, to hear our harmonious voices. Our songs ring out to glorify and honor our Lord and God. And as we sing the joyous sounds of saving grace, our choruses resonate for all those who will hear.

To the music of the ten-stringed lyre and the melody of the harp. (Psalm 92:3)

From Monday morning until Friday evening and then through Saturday soccer games and fishing trips, we encounter a Savior who is ever present with us. We face all the challenges of the week prayerfully and then see God's mighty hand at work in everything we put our hands to do. Then, those who God has brought into His eternal rest can rest from their labor and gather to exalt Him

---

2 "Amazing Grace" published in 1779. Lyrics by Anglican clergyman and poet John Newton (1725–1807). Public domain.
3 Psalm 119:54.
4 Psalm 33:9, Colossians 1:16.

because of His mighty works. When we enthusiastically sing out with praise, those who have occasioned to join us see and hear a powerful witness of the Word at work in our lives.

For you make me glad by your deeds, Lord; I sing for joy at what your hands have done. (Psalm 92:4)

It's so easy to get caught up in the daily grind and become ensnared in the corporate jungle. The world's noise and chaos try to drown out all that our heavenly Father accomplishes around us.

What God has done on our behalf is greater than words can express. The result of His power and wisdom are of great significance in our lives. His mighty acts are beyond what we can comprehend. As we come to worship before Jesus Christ our High Priest, we bow down in reverent awe to worship from our spirit as the Spirit leads.

True worship enthrones Christ as Lord of our lives and opens people's eyes to see all that God has done. Genuine worship, service, and ministry in Jesus' name profoundly affects all who gather with us.

How great are your works, Lord, how profound your thoughts! (Psalm 92:5)

We abandon our foolish ways when God's Word brings us to our senses. The correction of the Scriptures keeps us from affirming those who are lukewarm in their faith and apathetic about abiding in Christ. Halfhearted Christians may object to being admonished, saying, "I've been baptized, and I take communion. My religious obligations are fulfilled. I'll see you next Christmas." They disregard their Father, who longs for worship and sweet fellowship.

Occasional Christians have little desire for God's work in their lives except when they're in trouble. Christians in name only feel settled and self-satisfied with external religious practices and will not allow anyone to upset them in their complacency. They're a great mission field.

Senseless people do not know, fools do not understand, that though the wicked spring up like grass and all evildoers flourish, they will be destroyed forever. (Psalm 92:6–7)

We gather to hear God's Word taught and preached so that we may become fruitful in God's kingdom. We take the Spirit's instructions to heart, so we need not fear those who come against us with curses, threats, and insults. We know their end and resolve to remain in Christ, whose righteousness is everlasting. We stand on the Rock, who is Christ Jesus. He is forever and ever, the faithful witness, the Amen.[5]

---

5 Revelation 3:14.

We praise the Lord for He has created all the heavens and earth with its great sea creatures in the ocean's depths. He commands the lightning, hail, snow, and clouds to do His bidding. In His presence the mountains and hills flourish with mighty cedars. Great oak trees array the fields and forest. The countryside abounds with fruit trees that feed the wild animals, cattle, small creatures, and flying birds so they may flourish.[6] Come, see that the Lord is good and give witness to the beauty, majesty, and glory of His creation.

But you, Lord, are forever exalted.
(Psalm 92:8)

How does God—who is above all, our Savior who has overcome all, and the Spirit who strengthens us—make His name known among every tribe, nation, and language? This is the work of the church. We, the church, are called to go in the power of the Spirit and in the authority of Jesus' name to proclaim His vicarious death until He comes.

When we're arrested, the judge will hear of God's power to save. When we're called on the carpet, the boss will see the power of the Almighty's great mercies at work in our lives. When the Lord Almighty rescues His sons and daughters from powers of darkness, those who rule in strongholds and stand against Christ will see and know God's eternal purpose at work in and through us. These are mighty works that inspire us to sing out and speak out about God who is mighty to save.

His intent was that now, through the church, the manifold wisdom of God should be made known to the rulers and authorities in the heavenly realms, according to his eternal purpose that he accomplished in Christ Jesus our Lord.
(Ephesians 3:10–11)

Declaring God, who is mighty to save, is a major challenge when you're caught up in the entanglements of the corporate jungle. Deadlines, quotas, and workloads wear us down until we have little left to give. After dinner we pick up our remote and shut everything else out. We live in an online world that isolates us. There's no time to talk to the guy next door because we have a thousand friends on social media. We don't even have to go to the grocery store and stand in line with our neighbors. Just a few clicks and food shows up at our door.

We can't reach our friends and neighbors through social media alone. Volumes of emails just add to life's clutter of information. Online media is impersonal. There's a slim chance they will show up our church's door. What people really

---

6 Psalm 148:5—10.

need is a personal connection, increasingly difficult in an online world. This work of the Great Commission is especially important in our day because Christ has been hidden from whole generations.Come, let us stand and lift our voices in harmony with the Great I AM and speak out to this lost generation so they may hear and see God's mighty arm and outstretched hand at work on behalf of His people.

> Preach the word; be prepared in season and out of season; correct, rebuke and encourage—with great patience and careful instruction. (2 Timothy 4:2)

Chapter 26 Q&A

Declare His Mighty Works

1. Why are worship songs, hymns, and spiritual songs such powerful means of declaring what an awesome God we serve?

_____

_____

_____

2. How can we witness to people in an online world?

_____

_____

_____

3. What is one of the church's greatest mission fields?

_____

_____

_____

4. When we're called on the carpet at work, is this a time for fear or an opportunity to shine out with God's mighty work in our lives?

_____

_____

_____

My Journey's Journal:

Chapter 27: Obey the Gospel

Key Scriptures:

- "If you love me, keep my commands." (John 14:15)

- "We also have the prophetic message as something completely reliable, and you will do well to pay attention to it, as to a light shining in a dark place, until the day dawns and the morning star rises in your hearts." (2 Peter 1:19)

The rising sun awakens the dawn as it pierces the horizon. But the brightening light is just the beginning of a new day. "From the rising of the sun to the place where it sets, the name of the Lord is to be praised."[1] From the time we set our feet on the floor in the morning until we retire for the night, we walk in the light of our heavenly Father's love so we may delight in the fear of the Lord just as Jesus did.[2] Even in the night hours, God's Word is the theme of our song.[3] Every moment of every day we bask in the light of the bright morning star,[4] and at night we remember His name.[5]

Obeying the gospel isn't one moment of decision that changes our eternal destiny. We are set free from the curse of the law and called to obey the gospel of Jesus Christ. We have been forgiven of so much, and now our love of Christ compels us to obey His commands. Maturing Christians search the Scriptures so they may know what is right, just, and good. We're diligent students of God's Word so that we may act justly, love mercy, and walk humbly with our God.[6] As we walk in the light of gospel, we are reflections of Christ so that others may see Him and glorify His holy name.

> A prayer according to 1 Peter 4:17:
>
> Oh, God of justice, strengthen us to walk in the fear of the Lord, knowing your just and righteous judgments begin in your very own household. Make us grow strong in our faith so we may tenderly warn those who do not submit to the gospel's commands.

What a blessed moment when Jesus knocks on our heart's door and gifts us with the faith to receive Him as Lord and Savior. He makes us new creations

---

1 Psalm 113:3.
2 Isaiah 11:34.
3 Psalm 119:54.
4 Revelation 22:16.
5 Psalm 119:55.
6 Micah 6:8.

in Christ—new babies in the faith who need to be fed so we may grow and bear good fruit. Then we're baptized, but this isn't a one-time event. We must continue to live in keeping with our baptism.

Repentance isn't a stand-alone moment. Good deeds are the fruit of true repentance,[7] in the same way that evil deeds come from unrepentant hearts.[8] Partaking of the bread and cup at the Lord s Table renews our strength to live every day as partakers of Christ who indwells us. We are called to live in accordance with our baptism, make Jesus Lord of our everyday lives, abide in Christ continually, and drink from the cup of His suffering. We are saved by grace through faith and then strengthened in the faith so we may persist in doing good and seek God's glory and honor. These are essential elements of a Christian's daily life.

Fallible humans need constant reminders to seek first the kingdom of God and His righteousness. We need to be spiritually fed by the holy Scriptures as often as we sit down to feed our hungry bodies. Feeding on God's Word keeps us from forgetting the wonders of God's abundant grace and mercies. It's important to nourish our soul and spirit with the perfect law of freedom. We continue to feed on it so we may grow in grace and knowledge of Jesus Christ our Lord and Savior.

Do not merely listen to the word, and so deceive yourselves. Do what it says. Anyone who listens to the word but does not do what it says is like someone who looks at his face in a mirror and, after looking at himself, goes away and immediately forgets what he looks like. But whoever looks intently into the perfect law that gives freedom and continues in it—not forgetting what they have heard but doing it—they will be blessed in what they do.
(James 1:22–25)

Jesus didn't come to forgive and save us so we could follow our own rules and run amok. Christ's freedom is more like running free in our own backyard. He breaks the chains of our sin and gives us liberty to run on His narrow pathway.[9]

Consider the gospel's command that calls us to forgive those who have offended or harmed us. This truth is vital to a Christian's walk of faith, because when we offend our heavenly Father, then repent and ask for forgiveness, we'll be forgiven in the same way we forgive others. If we need God's mercy, we must show mercy. If we say we forgive but make those who offend us pay dearly for their wrong and keep reminding them of their faults, we will be forgiven in the same way.

Speak and act as those who are going to be judged by the law that gives freedom, because judgment without mercy will be shown to anyone who has not been merciful. Mercy triumphs over judgment.
(James 2:12–13)

---

7 Acts 26:20.
8 Hebrews 3:15—19.
9 Psalm 119:32.

188

The apostle Paul wrote many letters to strengthen and instruct the churches in all that is right and good so they could live according to love and keep the gospel's commands. He encouraged them to grasp hold of his teaching and follow his example just as he followed the example of Christ.[10] Paul established churches on his missionary journeys, revealing Christ to them by opening the holy Scriptures. Then he returned to confirm their faith, nurture, and admonish them in the Lord so their many trials would not weaken them.

So then, brothers and sisters, stand firm and hold fast to the teachings we passed on to you, whether by word of mouth or by letter.
(2 Thessalonians 2:15)

Too often Christian freedom is used as a defense to commit many wrongs. With this mindset, we soon become like God's people under the Old Testament Judges. "In those days Israel had no king; everyone did as they saw fit."[11] Can you hear the voices of lament? Yahweh was not King of people's lives. They went their own way, acting violently and causing grief. God's chosen nation waffled between idolatry, rebellion, and repentance. When they turned from their sin, Yahweh sent another judge to rescue them from their enemies.

In the same way, when Jesus Christ is not Lord of a Christian's life, we will neglect the gospel's commands and make up our own rules. We'll do what is right in our own eyes and wander into a valley of deep chaos and oppression.

You, my brothers and sisters, were called to be free. But do not use your freedom to indulge the flesh; rather, serve one another humbly in love.
(Galatians 5:13)

The gospel proclaims the perfect law of freedom. This freedom becomes a daily reality in our lives by means of the love of Christ who loved us first.[12] This perfect freedom liberates our hearts to love our wives as Christ loved the church.[13] We're set free to love our neighbors as ourselves.[14] This liberty makes it possible to thrive as living sacrifices and, "Love your enemies, do good to those who hate you, bless those who curse you, and pray for those who spitefully use you."[15]

You, my brothers and sisters, were called to be free. But do not use your freedom to indulge the flesh; rather, serve one another humbly in love. For the entire law is fulfilled in keeping this one command: "Love your neighbor as yourself."
(Galatians 5:13–14)

Obeying the law of love makes it possible to love unlovable people. Following Jesus' command to love makes it possible to love those who wrong us. The love of

---

10 1 Corinthians 11:1.
11 Judges 17:6, 21:25.
12 1 John 4:19.
13 Ephesians 5:25.
14 Matthew 22:39.
15 Luke 6:27—28.

Christ inspires us to lend to those who cannot pay us back. In the love of Christ, we can invite a family to dinner knowing they can't afford to do the same for our family. We can be kind to those who never say, "thank you." Jesus' commands compel us to show mercy in the same way our heavenly Father shows mercy.[16] The law of love sets us free to love liberally.

> *The goal of this command is love, which comes from a pure heart and a good conscience and a sincere faith.*
> (1 Timothy 1:5)

Consider God's chosen nation as they wavered between obedience to the Law and following what they thought was right for themselves in the moment. The chaos they caused by exalting themselves as their own gods and following false gods was dreadful—a story of horrors.[17]

The record of Israel's history was written to warn and teach us. They turned away from God and we can see the consequences. We read about them calling out to Yahweh for help, repenting of their sins. We see God restoring His blessings upon the nation. Their lives teach us so that "through the endurance taught in the Scriptures and the encouragement they provide we might have hope."[18]

We're not subject to the Old Testament Law. Jesus fulfilled every word and punctuation mark in the Law.[19] Now we are called to a higher standard. The Mosaic Law said, "an eye for an eye and a tooth for a tooth," but the gospel calls us to turn the other cheek and repay evil by doing good in turn.[20] In Christ, we are set free from the curse of the Law. The gospel's higher standard crushes us and reveals our need of Christ and His righteousness that He imparts to us as our own. We are forgiven, cleansed, and made right with the Father so that we delight to obey from the heart.

> *But thanks be to God that, though you used to be slaves to sin, you have come to obey from your heart the pattern of teaching that has now claimed your allegiance.*
> (Romans 6:17)

A child's first breath is a moment of joy that anticipates a life full of vitality accompanied by many breaths. When we hear, and believe the gospel's life-giving message and receive the gift of faith, this is a good beginning for a lifelong walk of faithfulness. By the power of the word, in the waters of baptism, we die

---

16 Luke 6:32—36.
17 Judges 19:22—29.
18 Romans 15:4.
19 Matthew 5:18.
20 Matthew 5:38—42, 1 Peter 3:9.

190

to ourselves and are buried with Christ. We are raised from the baptismal waters in resurrection power and united with the Father, Son, and Holy Spirit. Then, our feet are ready on the starting line. We leap from our starting point to run the race—a life of obedience to the gospel and walking in the fear of the Lord.[21]

> The fear of the Lord is the beginning of wisdom; all who follow his precepts have good understanding. To him belongs eternal praise. (Psalm 111:10)

Chapter 27 Q&A

Obey the Gospel

1. Why is obeying the gospel more than a one-time event?

_____

_____

_____

2. Why are we often conflicted between Christian freedom and being conformed to Christ?

_____

_____

_____

3. How does the Good News affect a Christian's daily life?

_____

_____

_____

4. How is it possible to live up to the gospel's impossible standard?

_____

_____

_____

5. What good purpose does it serve for us to read Israel's history?

_____

_____

_____

---

21 Definition of "Fear of the Lord" is reverent submission, awe, and delighted obedience. (Hebrews 5:7, Hebrews 12:28, Isaiah 11:3.)

My Journey's Journal:

Chapter 28: Confirming the Gospel

Key Scriptures:

- "So Paul and Barnabas spent considerable time there, speaking boldly for the Lord, who confirmed the message of his grace by enabling them to perform signs and wonders" (Acts 14:3).

- "After the Lord Jesus had spoken to them, he was taken up into heaven and he sat at the right hand of God. Then the disciples went out and preached everywhere, and the Lord worked with them and confirmed his word by the signs that accompanied it" (Mark 16:19–20).

When you raise and train a thoroughbred racehorse, there comes a time when you must prove what you've been bragging about. Big talk never wins a race. You must put a jockey on the horse and put your four-year-old steed on the starting line. Then he charges out of the gates to prove your claims.

We live in a time when Christ's grace and forgiveness have been hidden from so many in an entire generation. There's a famine of hearing God's Word that has spread like a creeping darkness throughout the world.[1] The times we live in are much like the days when the church was first established. The early church proclaimed the gospel to people who lived under a shadow of darkness in pagan cultures. The Spirit of Christ performed signs and wonders to prove the gospel's message.

Consider the challenges we face as we minister to this generation. Most schools teach that we evolved from fossil organisms. It's a rare moment if our children hear of Creator God or a risen Savior who loves and forgives. Great American universities began as pillars of Christian faith but now crush any faith a freshman may have.

Because of this, Christ's messengers must prove that what they say is true and real—more than made-up words of their own. Our Savior's ambassadors must continue to testify under the authority of Christ and in the power of the Holy Spirit until the work of the church is finished. They are called to act by the Spirit's leading to provide undeniable signs and wonders to people who are uncertain about a Savior they can't see. They have never heard of His mercies and saving grace. The people around us are clueless about what it means to

---

1 Amos 8:11.

run the race marked before us[2] and they need Christ revealed to them in a tangible way.

A prayer according to John 6:26:

Oh, Lord and Savior, open the eyes of this generation so we may look to Christ our Redeemer who proves the truth of the Good News with loving acts.

Jesus taught the people with authority.[3] He didn't speak His own words but what the Father commanded Him to say.[4] Every word He spoke and every miracle He performed was exactly what the Father was speaking and doing.[5] Jesus brought light to a people walking in darkness.[6] His words had authority, and He backed them up with proof of His power and might to save. He radiated with light to drive back the darkness and then rose with healing in His wings.[7] He spoke life-giving truths with powerful words and then reached out His hands with a miraculous touch that proved His words true.

Jesus replied, "Go back and report to John what you hear and see: The blind receive sight, the lame walk, those who have leprosy are cleansed, the deaf hear, the dead are raised, and the good news is proclaimed to the poor. Blessed is anyone who does not stumble on account of me."
(Matthew 11:4–6)

Jesus, the Word of all creation, performed His first miracle at a wedding in Cana, a town in Galilee. The hour had come for Jesus to reveal Himself as Messiah and to manifest His glory. He turned water into wine, and it was better than the first wine offered to the guests.

Jesus taught the first five disciples and proved His words with signs. All twelve disciples heard Jesus' words and followed Him. Then they saw many manifestations of the glory of Christ as confirmations of their faith.

What Jesus did here in Cana of Galilee was the first of the signs through which he revealed his glory; and his disciples believed in him.
(John 2:11)

Jesus, (Yeshua) came as Immanuel, God with us. No man gave Him this name. The Father gave it to Him, and it powerfully manifests in His living and active presence. The power of His name and His presence have not diminished over time. God has not changed. He still rises with healing in His wings.

Religious traditions blinded some of the pharisees. Others grudgingly believed that God was *with* Jesus. A few thought He was a great teacher. Many of

---

2 Hebrews 12:1.
3 Matthew 7:29.
4 John 12:49.
5 John 15:19.
6 Isaiah 9:2, Matthew 4:16.
7 Malachi 4:2.

the people considered Him to be a prophet. But the truth is that Yeshua was fully man and fully God—God manifested in the flesh to dwell among us and then ascend to the right hand of the Father.[8]

We are sent to testify of God's saving grace, but not with words alone. We are sent to minister and serve under authority so we may do our work for the cause of Christ and the cross. We speak with authority because we do not speak our own words but our Father's words. Truth and righteousness are the touchstone for every word we speak. In the power of His holy name, we speak out with God's Word and then reach out our hands to minister, doing what we see our Father doing, touching those whom we see our Savior touching.

> *He came to Jesus at night and said, "Rabbi, we know that you are a teacher who has come from God. For no one could perform the signs you are doing if God were not with him."*
> (John 3:2)

Is our testimony of Jesus Christ with words alone? John, the baptizer, called people to repent and be baptized and then announced the Messiah to the crowds saying, "Behold, the Lamb of God, who takes away the sin of the world!"[9] Jesus began His ministry with a miracle—changing water into wine. He taught His disciples and proved His words with signs and wonders.

Christians are called to serve as witnesses of their Lord and Savior, Jesus Christ. Our testimony begins with words that are then proven with action. The first proof of what we say is living in keeping with truth in our homes, neighborhoods, and on the job. Then, when we do our part in the work of the Great Commission according to the spiritual gifts given to us, this is a great testimony of saving grace that performed a good work in our heart and soul.

We offer further proof when we minister, serve, and worship in the spirit and according to truth. When people see us go through trials that can't break us, this proves the genuineness of our faith, and they get a glimpse of Christ. When people see us love our enemies, they see our Redeemer's love. It's a great testimony when the joy of our salvation overflows when hard times test our faith.[10]

> *"I have testimony weightier than that of John. For the works that the Father has given me to finish–the very works that I am doing–testify that the Father has sent me."*
> (John 5:36)

When the church extends their hands as the very hand of Christ, this is proof that the gospel message is true and real. Signs and wonders confirm that the truth is taught, preached, and believed. Manifestations and workings of spiritual

---

8 1 Timothy 3:16.
9 John 1:29.
10 1 Peter 1:6—9.

gifts are evidence of the true gospel at work in the church.[11] Miracles and ministries in gifts of the Spirit wake people up to the reality of Christ. Then saving faith comes by hearing God's Word, and their hearing is made possible by the power of the Word ministered by the Holy Spirit.[12]

The crowds looked to Jesus with awe because He taught with authority. Then He proved His teaching to be true by reaching out His hands to forgive, heal the sick, make the lame walk, give hearing to the deaf, give seeing eyes to the blind, and raise the dead to life.

Still, many in the crowd believed in him. They said, "When the Messiah comes, will he perform more signs than this man?"
(John 7:31)

There are many proofs to confirm that we have heard, received, and believed the true gospel message by faith in Jesus Christ. The primary proof is that we become greater reflections of Christ. Our hearts and minds become Christ saturated.

We don't have to work through ten, twelve, or twenty steps and then we're saved. We are saved by grace and through faith alone. Christ produces evidence of our faith. He grafts us into the Vine to be branches that produce good fruit.

A good sign of our faith is Christ overflowing to everyone around us. Doing good things does not save us. Being the hardest working servant in the church can't redeem us. But when we are fruitful in Christ, the people around us can't help but notice what we do in Jesus' name, and they are drawn to Christ who indwells us.

Jesus answered, "I did tell you, but you do not believe. The works I do in my Father's name testify about me, but you do not believe because you are not my sheep.
(John 10:25–26)

When you express your love to your spouse, it's best to prove it with action. Just saying it, because that's what couples do, but never backing it up with deeds makes your words sound hallow. What you do is proof of what you say.

Jesus made a bold claim before His disciples. Speaking of Himself, he said, "This is the bread that came down from heaven"[13] If these words are too hard to accept on their own merit, then let your eyes see what Christ's living and active presence accomplishes among His people today. If what Immanuel taught with His words does not persuade you, then let His mighty hand and outstretched arm convince you that His words are spirit and life.[14]

---

11 Acts 14:3.
12 Romans 10:17.
13 John 6:58.
14 John 6:63.

"But if I do them, even though you do not believe me, believe the works, that you may know and understand that the Father is in me, and I in the Father."
(John 10:38)

Politicians make a lot of promises when campaigning for your vote. They get elected because they guaranteed "a chicken in every pot and a car in every garage."[15] But if they don't deliver what they promise, the pots and garages remain empty, like the politician's words. Hoover's promise turned into many shanty towns often called Hoovervilles that sprang up during the Great Depression.

Words, creeds, confessions, songs, and testimonials that do not prove true in acts of ministry and service are not very convincing. The church has a provable, life-giving message in the gospel. We preach the Good News of Jesus Christ and the cross with power and authority and prove it by our deeds. The Spirit of Christ gives good gifts to the church so we may offer proof of the gospel's veracity.

But if we only speak words and take no action, we are not very convincing. Jesus' living and active presence is there with us as we gather to worship as a church. He has given us good gifts and the authority of His name to minister to others. We serve according to the gifts of the Spirit to prove that we speak the true gospel. Jesus extends His hands, using our hands to reach out and touch those who are drawn by His words of life and liberty.

God also testified to it [message of salvation] by signs, wonders and various miracles, and by gifts of the Holy Spirit distributed according to his will.
(Hebrews 2:4)

Everybody has words to speak. Some more than others. A candidate for public office speaks with inspiring promises of what he will do for the people. A great general's words inspire his troops, challenging them to fight for their homeland. A teacher's words inspire her students to learn.

But political ambitions often make a man's words worthless. A general that is all talk and no fight wins no battles. A teacher who inspires learning but offers no instruction leaves a void in a student's education. Words are meaningless unless they're proven by acts that back them up. Love is hollow if it is only words. Jesus said, "The kingdom of God has come near. Repent and believe the good news!" Then He backed up His words by casting out an impure spirit.[16]

Now while he was in Jerusalem at the Passover Festival, many people saw the signs he was performing and believed in his name. (John 2:23)

15 Herbert Hoover, 1928 presidential campaign slogan.
16 Mark 1:15—25.

Chapter 28 Q&A

Confirming the Gospel

1. How are people in our day like the generation of the early church?

_____

_____

_____

2. If the modern-day church is well established, why is proof of the gospel necessary?

_____

_____

_____

3. How do we know that the power and authority of Jesus' name is the same as it was two thousand years ago?

_____

_____

_____

4. What proof can Christians offer in their daily lives to those in need of Christ?

_____

_____

_____

5. Do signs, wonders, and miracles alone turn a person's heart toward Christ?

_____

_____

_____

My Journey's Journal:

Chapter 29: Making Disciples

Key Scriptures:

- "Then Jesus came to them and said, 'All authority in heaven and on earth has been given to me. Therefore go and make disciples of all nations, baptizing them in the name of the Father and of the Son and of the Holy Spirit, and teaching them to obey everything I have commanded you. And surely I am with you always, to the very end of the age'" (Matthew 28:18-20).

- "So Christ himself gave the apostles, the prophets, the evangelists, the pastors and teachers, to equip his people for works of service, so that the body of Christ may be built up until we all reach unity in the faith and in the knowledge of the Son of God and become mature, attaining to the whole measure of the fullness of Christ" (Ephesians 4:11–13).

If you send your son or daughter on a hunting trip without helping them prepare, it could end in disaster. A spontaneous family camping trip without getting ready often leads to chaos. A person who gets up in front of a classroom without an education that prepares them to organize and teach a lesson, often wastes his student's time. Knowledge, apprenticeship, and preparation are required whether you work as a plumber, a doctor, or an ambassador of Christ.

Because Jesus Christ has all authority in heaven and earth, we who are in Christ are called to go and serve by the authority of his name. By His command we speak out God's gospel message with authority to make disciples and equip them to serve. The Spirit of Christ provides the church with gifted apostles, prophets, evangelists, pastors, and teachers who guide God's people by leading them into the fullness of Christ to prepare and empower them for the work of the Great Commission.

> A prayer according to Colossians 3:16:
>
> Oh, Lord of the harvest, may the message of Christ dwell among us richly so we may teach and admonish each other according to all wisdom with psalms, hymns, and spiritual songs; speaking and singing out with gratitude from our hearts.

When you build a house, the work isn't finished until you drive the final nail and paint the last wall. A house isn't really a home until the family moves in to fill the rooms with laughter. Building house and home begins with planning and preparation. Then the job is finally accomplished with a lot of sacrifice and hard work.

201

Building the church is not complete until the gospel is heard on every continent, island, and in every jungle tribe on earth. There is still work to do until the church gathers a "great multitude that no one could count, from every nation, tribe, people and language."[1] If you look forward to Christ's return, you can "hasten the day" by doing your part in the work of the Great Commission.[2]

> *And this gospel of the kingdom will be preached in the whole world as a testimony to all nations, and then the end will come.*
> (Matthew 24:14)

Consider the joy of getting prepared and then sent out to preach and minister in Jesus' holy name. Jesus sent the twelve apostles under the authority of His name. He also sent seventy-two disciples to serve under authority to heal the sick and tell them "the kingdom of God has come near you."[3] They came back rejoicing in all that the Lord had done through them.

Jesus sent the twelve and then seventy-two to proclaim Good News to those who walked in darkness. Now the mission expands with more and more disciples and followers needing to be discipled and then sent out. The seventy-two could only reach Galilee and Judea with their message. Now the church is charged with the task of going to the entire world, with a population of over eight billion people.

How can the church accomplish this impossible job? Getting organized, prepared, and planning is necessary, but organized religion is rarely effective when it comes to sending ambassadors of Christ. Religion divides us in our mission, but Christ unites.[4] We don't take an organization or denomination to the world. We lift up Christ so that He will draw all men.[5] Religious organizations may focus on digging wells for drinking water, while ambassadors of Christ provide water wells and announce Christ, the water of life.

> *The seventy-two returned with joy and said, "Lord, even the demons submit to us in your name." He replied, "I saw Satan fall like lightning from heaven. I have given you authority to trample on snakes and scorpions and to overcome all the power of the enemy; nothing will harm you. However, do not rejoice that the spirits submit to you, but rejoice that your names are written in heaven."*
> (Luke 10:17–20)

Our heavenly Father sent His only Son to dwell among us and then serve as a ransom for sin. He anointed Jesus to proclaim Good News to the poor and freedom for prisoners. God sent His only Son to restore sight to the blind, set the oppressed free, and proclaim the year of the Lord's favor.[6]

1 Revelation 7:9.
2 2 Peter 3:12.
3 Luke 10:9.
4 Religion is a search for God. But the truth is that Christ searches for us while we are dead in our sins.
5 John 12:32. The Greek word for "men" means; each, every, any, all, the whole, everyone, all things, everything collectively.
6 Luke 4:18—19.

Now, Jesus sends out ransomed souls just as the Father sent Him. Indeed, those who believe in Jesus as Lord and Savior are the church, called to do greater things.[7] When the Holy Spirit opens our eyes and reveals Christ, we can see what Christ has done for us. He died in our place, for our sins, and the sins of the world.

How is Jesus sending us? In the same way the Father sent Him. We are called to do the same work Jesus did. We give up our own glory—our own way of life— so we may serve the cause of Christ and the cross. Our own strength and authority count for nothing.[8] The words we speak on our own have no power. Jesus' sends us by the power and authority of His holy name.

Again Jesus said, "Peace be with you! As the Father has sent me, I am sending you." And with that he breathed on them and said, "Receive the Holy Spirit. If you forgive anyone's sins, their sins are forgiven; if you do not forgive them, they are not forgiven." (John 20:21–23)

Prepared and empowered witnesses are necessary in the work of the Great Commission. If the apostle Peter had stood before the crowds in Jerusalem to speak his own words, by his own authority, or by means of his own charisma, thousands of people would have gone home the same way they came. Instead, he spoke to the pressing crowds after receiving the anointing fire of the Holy Spirit. He boldly proclaimed Christ crucified for the sins of the world. Then three thousand people believed in Jesus Christ as Savior and were baptized the same day.

Like Peter, we need knowledge, training, discipling, *and* the anointing work of the Holy Spirit so we may take the Good News to our neighbors and coworkers. Jesus taught His disciples for over three years at Jesus University and then said, "I am going to send you what my Father has promised; but stay in the city until you have been clothed with power from on high."[9] In the same way, we must be discipled and then wait on the Lord, who clothes us with the Holy Spirit's power, so we may step out to do the work of the church. What we build requires a foundation. We need the knowledge of Christ to accompany our zeal for the gospel, so we can build upon the Rock. If we do not submit to God's righteousness, have little knowledge of Christ, and don't wait for the Spirit's fire, we cannot be effective in the work of the Great Commission.[10]

"But you will receive power when the Holy Spirit comes on you; and you will be my witnesses in Jerusalem, and in all Judea and Samaria, and to the ends of the earth." (Acts 1:8)

We are sent out with knowledge and a powerful means of grace. The Holy Spirit empowers the Word in us. Every word we speak comes from the word that the Spirit of Christ breathed into the hearts and minds of the inspired

7 John 14:12.
8 Philippians 3:8.
9 Luke 24:49.
10 Romans 10:2—3.

203

writers of the Scriptures. We lift a banner who is Christ, doing our part as He draws all people.[11]

Then we make disciples of those who hear and believe God's promise of redemption through Jesus Christ. We prepare converts by instructing, admonishing, nurturing, and schooling them in all righteousness. After they are equipped for the work, they still need the empowering work of the Holy Spirit. We fast, pray, and lay holy hands on them and send them out to raise Christ's banner before their neighbors and the nations.[12]

All Scripture is God-breathed and is useful for teaching, rebuking, correcting and training in righteousness, so that the servant of God may be thoroughly equipped for every good work.
(2 Timothy 3:16–17)

Has the post modern church come into the "unity in the faith and in the knowledge of the Son of God?" Have all Christians "become mature, attaining to the whole measure of the fullness of Christ?"[13] It's obvious we have not! That means we have a lot of discipling left to do. Has the gospel been preached to every tribe, nation, and in every language? Not yet! That means the church still needs to make disciples who are prepared and sent to announce Christ's Jubilee.

Because the work is not yet complete, the church must prepare and send ambassadors to proclaim and prove the gospel that offers forgiveness and saves lost souls. The proof is placed in the hands we extend as the hands of Christ to touch, heal the sick, open the eyes of the blind, make the lame walk, and set the oppressed free from the chains of sin. This is not possible in our own strength but in the dynamos of the Spirit of Christ who works in and through us.

He is the one we proclaim, admonishing and teaching everyone with all wisdom, so that we may present everyone fully mature in Christ. To this end I strenuously contend with all the energy Christ so powerfully works in me.
(Colossians 1:28–29)

Prepare, practice, repeat. After we are brought to saving faith in Jesus Christ, it's vital that we submit to being discipled and prepared so we may serve as ambassadors. Schooling is necessary before being sent to proclaim, "The kingdom of God has come near you." If we go out untrained and on our own, we walk a perilous path. We're unworthy messengers if we speak our own words in our own way and by our own means.

11 John 12:32.
12 Acts 13:3.
13 Ephesians 4:13.

How then do we go about fulfilling the impossible work of the Great Commission? We are taught so we may learn the truths of the Scriptures and grow in grace and knowledge. Then maturing believers serve to guide and nurture new believers. Taking time to practice defending our faith is a vital discipline for all who give testimony of God's mighty work of saving grace. Then, before we are sent to neighbor and nations, the elders or presbyters of the church fast, pray, and lay holy hands on us in Jesus' name to gift and empower us with the fire of the Holy Spirit for the good work of our calling in Jesus Christ.

Their fervent prayers compel the Spirit of Jesus to fill our heart with fire of the Word that we cannot hold back.[14] We make disciples by giving them knowledge of Christ. Then the anointing, gifting, and empowering work of the Spirit imparts a fiery zeal to proclaim Christ's vicarious death, baptize those who receive and believe, and make disciples until the day Christ returns to take us to our forever home.

> He told them, "This is what is written: The Messiah will suffer and rise from the dead on the third day, and repentance for the forgiveness of sins will be preached in his name to all nations, beginning at Jerusalem. You are witnesses of these things. I am going to send you what my Father has promised; but stay in the city until you have been clothed with power from on high." (Luke 24:46–49)

---

14 Jeremiah 20:9.

Chapter 29 Q&A

Making Disciples

1. How many harvest workers are needed to reach eight billion people?

_____

_____

_____

2. What does the way God sent His only Son teach us about how we are sent?

_____

_____

_____

3. What made the difference in Peter before Pentecost and then on the day of Pentecost?

_____

_____

_____

4. How does a church go about preparing and sending ambassadors of Christ to neighbors and nations?

_____

_____

_____

My Journey's Journal:

Sent to Raise Christ's Banner

Before ascending to the right hand of the Father, Jesus commanded His followers to "Go and make disciples of all nations." This is a mountain-sized command with monumental challenges. Sending us out to raise Christ's banner before all tribes and every homeland gives us a job that is unattainable by means of our own strength and abilities. The prophet Zechariah makes this clear as he proclaims the words the Lord spoke to him: "'Not by might nor by power, but by my Spirit,' says the Lord Almighty."[1] The original Hebrew amplifies the truth that neither human might nor common strength can accomplish the work. We need the power authority of Jesus' name that only comes from above.

We must be taught and trained to be effective fishermen before being sent to neighbors and nations to proclaim Christ and the cross. We need to be discipled before we go to baptize and make more disciples. The best practice is to learn to defend our faith in a safe environment at our home church. Being discipled keeps us faithful to become students of God's Word and grow in grace and knowledge of Christ and His redemptive work on the cross.

With prayer and fasting, church leaders serve as presbyters and lay their hands on us to impart the gifts of the Spirit according to His will. This preparation is necessary so that we can do the impossible work of the Great Commission made possible by the Spirit of grace.

The gospel we proclaim and the baptisms we perform are not just common words or the ideas of men. They are God's word and the power of His name proven eternally true and real by various manifestations of the Spirit of Christ. When lost souls come to saving faith in a living Savior, we baptize them into the Father, Son, and Holy Spirit through water and by the Word. As they go down into the water and raised up from the water, they die with Christ, are buried with Christ, and raised up in resurrection power with Christ.

Spiritual gifts given for ministry and service in the work of the church provide further proof of our salvation.[2] Miraculous signs and wonders that He performs among the people also provide a witness of God's saving grace. Where the gospel message is heard, believed, and received, the Holy Spirit confirms the Good News as true with mighty acts. This is the great salvation we are called to proclaim to neighbors and nations.

It's an incredible delight to be given a job that is impossible and then see what God accomplishes through us by the anointing, gifting, and empowering work of

1 Zechariah 4:6.
2 1 Corinthians 1:6—7.

the Holy Spirit. When we are given a task, we take an account of ourselves and realize that we don't have what the job requires. Then by the power of the Word and the work of the Spirit we are refined, molded, and shaped into useful vessels for God's kingdom so that we may raise Christ's banner for all to see.

We are sent to proclaim Christ in the same way Jesus was sent. He came in humility and manifested the power and authority of God's holy name. And yet, Jesus declared that His church would do greater even things. The apostle Paul followed in Jesus' footsteps and proclaimed Christ to the people in weakness, fear of the Lord, and with much trembling.[3]

Ambassadors of God's kingdom come to serve with their human frailties. The Spirit empowers them to teach and declare God's Word to reveal Christ and open the eyes of those who are spiritually blind. Witnesses of God's saving grace speak what the Word is speaking and reach out their hands to touch those whom Jesus touches. We give up our personal ambitions to take up the mantle of a servant so we may serve in the cause of Christ and the cross. We raise a banner for the nations and God moves mountains to make straight the way for us to accomplish the impossible work of Jesus' Great Commission.[4]

> Now to him who is able to establish you in accordance with my gospel, the message I proclaim about Jesus Christ, in keeping with the revelation of the mystery hidden for long ages past, but now revealed and made known through the prophetic writings by the command of the eternal God, so that all Gentiles might come to the obedience that comes from faith—to the only wise God be glory forever through Jesus Christ! Amen. (Romans 16:25–27)

---

3 1 Corinthians 2:3.
4 John 1:23.

Milton Keynes UK
Ingram Content Group UK Ltd.
UKHW020806080424
440801UK00014B/716